CHANGING
CHURCH

PUBLISHED BY REGAL BOOKS
FROM GOSPEL LIGHT
VENTURA, CALIFORNIA, U.S.A.
PRINTED IN THE U.S.A.

Regal

Regal Books is a ministry of Gospel Light, a Christian publisher dedicated to serving the local church. We believe God's vision for Gospel Light is to provide church leaders with biblical, user-friendly materials that will help them evangelize, disciple and minister to children, youth and families.

It is our prayer that this Regal book will help you discover biblical truth for your own life and help you meet the needs of others. May God richly bless you.

For a free catalog of resources from Regal Books/Gospel Light, please call your Christian supplier or contact us at 1-800-4-GOSPEL *or* www.regalbooks.com.

Cover design by David Griffing

Library of Congress Cataloging-in-Publication Data

Wagner, C. Peter.
  Changing Church / C. Peter Wagner.
    p. cm.
  Includes bibliographical references (p.   ) and index.
  ISBN 0-8307-3278-0 (hardcover); 0-8307-3658-1 (trade paperback)
  1. Christianity—Forecasting. 2. Church history—21st century. 3. Church history—20th century. I. Title.
  BR481.W23 2004
  270.8'3'0112—dc22   2004004378

1 2 3 4 5 6 7 8 9 10 11 12 13 14 15 / 10 09 08 07 06 05 04

Rights for publishing this book in other languages are contracted by Gospel Light Worldwide, the international nonprofit ministry of Gospel Light. Gospel Light Worldwide also provides publishing and technical assistance to international publishers dedicated to producing Sunday School and Vacation Bible School curricula and books in the languages of the world. For additional information, visit www.gospellightworldwide.org; write to Gospel Light Worldwide, P.O. Box 3875, Ventura, CA 93006; or send an e-mail to info@gospellightworldwide.org.

CHANGING CHURCH

C. PETER WAGNER

Regal

From Gospel Light
Ventura, California, U.S.A.

CONTENTS

CHAPTER ONE

THE SECOND APOSTOLIC AGE

IN MANY WAYS THE YEAR 2001 WAS A SIGNIFICANT YEAR, NOT THE LEAST OF WHICH IS THAT IT MARKED THE BEGINNING OF THE SECOND APOSTOLIC AGE.

I am well aware of the fact that what I have said could be regarded as somewhat of a brash statement. Many would undoubtedly call into question my due respect for historiography. They might say, "How can you affirm that we are in a new age so soon? It ordinarily takes decades of dialogue and debate for historians to arrive at such a conclusion."

EXTRAORDINARY TIMES— EXTRAORDINARY CHANGE

My first response would be that we do not live in ordinary times—we live in extraordinary times. Changes are more rapid and more radical now than they ever have been. Consider, for example, that we have gone from VHS to CD to DVD in only a few brief years. These days, if we wait too long to recognize the importance of an innovation or if we postpone analyzing the ripple effects it may have on our society in general and on our lives in particular, the new thing may well pass us by.

This applies especially to the Church. Past generations had little need to be concerned about change. For example, traditionally Lutheran grandparents, parents and children could go to church together Sunday after Sunday with a deep and comfortable assurance that everything would pretty much be the same the next year or 10 years later. They operated on an unspoken assumption that Lutheranism would be the same yesterday, today and forever. This would also be true of Methodists, Baptists, Mennonites, Assemblies of God, Episcopalians or whomever.

But today things are not as they were. Many of the new churches that have been springing up would be almost unrecognizable to the generations of believers that have now passed off the scene. Today, few parents who belong to traditional churches are either surprised or upset when their children decide to join other, more contemporary churches. Even inside traditional churches themselves, many things—from dress codes to worship styles—are notably different from what they were as little as five years ago.

Change is now a fact of life. Rapid change. Radical change. Are you ready for this? If not, be careful. History may pass you by!

Now, let's take a closer look at the Second Apostolic Age.

THE NEW APOSTOLIC REFORMATION

We are now seeing before our very eyes the most radical change in the way of doing church since the Protestant Reformation. In fact, I think I could make a reasonable argument that it may actually turn out to be a *more radical* change. I am not referring to doctrinal change; nothing has or likely ever will match the profound doctrinal insights that the Reformers surfaced, such as the authority of Scripture, justification by faith and the priesthood of all believers. The changes we are currently experiencing leave essential doctrines like this intact while at the same time reengineer the way that churches operate and carry out their daily activities. Some call these churches "new churches," "ChurchNext," "new paradigm churches" or "postdenominational churches." Sociologist Donald E. Miller has titled his excellent book on the movement, *Reinventing American Protestantism* (University of California Press), because the reinvention of American Protestantism is precisely what seems to be happening.

The name I have chosen for this movement is the New Apostolic Reformation. I use "Reformation" because, as I have said, I believe it at least matches the Protestant Reformation in its overall impact; "Apostolic" because the most radical of all the changes is the widespread recognition of the gift and office of apostle in today's churches; and "New" to distinguish the movement from a number of denominations that use the word "Apostolic" in their official names yet exhibit patterns common to the more traditional churches rather than to these new ones.

The deepest influential roots of the New Apostolic Reformation can be traced back to the African Independent Church movement, which started around 1900 in Africa. The revelation of contemporary apostles and prophets can be traced farther back, at least as far back as Edward Irving of England in the 1830s. However, his movement, called the Irvingites, never became very influential. The American independent charismatic movement, which started about 1970, is another root of the New Apostolic Reformation. In China, the house church movement started in the mid-1970s after the Cultural Revolution. Likewise, the Latin American version, known as the grassroots church movement, dates back to the late 1970s.

Fed by these many roots, the New Apostolic Reformation came to fruition through prophecy, as might be expected according to Scripture: "Surely the Lord GOD does nothing, unless He reveals His secret to His servants the prophets" (Amos 3:7).

One of my closest prophetic colleagues for many years has been Bill Hamon of Christian International. In his book *The Eternal Church*, Hamon traces the history of the New Apostolic Reformation, which he calls the Prophetic-Apostolic Movement, and pinpoints an extraordinary visitation of the Holy Spirit in a meeting at the Sandestin Beach Resort Inn in Sandestin, Florida, on October 15, 1988. As he looks back on that experience, Hamon says, "God's timely purpose for His prophets was officially birthed into the Church world on October 15, 1988, and was launched into what has become known as the Prophetic-Apostolic Movement."[1]

It was in the 1990s, shortly after Hamon's prophetic word, that some began to notice that there were strong commonalities across the four movements that I have just described and that together they might be seen as an important new activity of the Holy Spirit in our midst.

In the historical flow of Christianity in the United States, it is helpful to see that the genealogy of the New Apostolic Reformation begins first with the classical Pentecostal movement and continues with the independent charismatic movement. However, the New Apostolic Reformation should not be regarded as exclusively charismatic. No one knows exactly, but a fair guess is that it might be comprised of 80 percent charismatic and 20 percent noncharismatic evangelicals.

INTERCESSORS, PROPHETS AND APOSTLES

As I have mentioned, the most radical characteristic of the New Apostolic Reformation is the widespread recognition that the office of apostle was not just a phenomenon of the first couple of centuries of church history but that it is also functioning in the Body of Christ today. The process leading up to this, at least in the United States, began in the late 1940s with a break-off movement from classical Pentecostalism to which some have given names like the "restoration movement," "healing evangelism" and "Latter Rain." One of the reasons this upstart movement was rejected by classical Pentecostals, such as the Assemblies of God, is that it affirmed the contemporary offices of apostle and prophet. The movement did not continue to gain strength for several reasons, perhaps in part because the time was not yet ripe.

As this early attempt at restoring the office of apostle began to lose momentum, it seems that the Holy Spirit initiated a sequence of innovations that have led us to where we are today. The first occurred in the 1970s, when the gift and office of intercessor began to be recognized by the Body of Christ; the second was in the 1980s, with the recognition of the gift and office of prophet; and the third was in the 1990s, with the gift and office of apostle. As would be expected, each one produced its share of discussion, debate and fine-tuning until, by the end of the century, a growing number of people were becoming comfortable with all three. This opened the door for a critical mass to develop by 2001, the year I have chosen to use as the beginning of the Second Apostolic Age.

I will be using the terms "New Apostolic Reformation" and "Second Apostolic Age" frequently throughout this book, so it might be helpful to clarify their meanings early on. The New Apostolic Reformation is the process of change in the Church that I have traced back to around 1900. I believe it will continue into the future for a sustained period of time. The Second Apostolic Age is a historical season, not a process. As a result of what God has been doing through the New Apostolic Reformation, we now find ourselves in the Second Apostolic Age. Many more details will be added, but this gives us a basic understanding of terminology.

I am well aware that large segments of the Body of Christ reject the notion that there could be biblical apostles today and that there is little or no chance that they will ever change their minds. Furthermore, even those of us who are inclined to affirm the office of apostle still have a long way to go: We need to work out kinks in our apostolic theology; we need to compile case studies of fruitful apostolic ministry; and we need to communicate our ideas with persuasiveness and integrity. I hope that, as we do, the ideas will gain acceptance in wider and wider circles of the constituency of the Church. If we now, in fact, have a true critical mass, these things are bound to materialize over time.

> THE MOST RADICAL CHARACTERISTIC OF
> THE NEW APOSTOLIC REFORMATION IS THE
> WIDESPREAD RECOGNITION THAT THE OFFICE
> OF APOSTLE IS FUNCTIONING IN THE
> BODY OF CHRIST TODAY.

THE SEQUENCE

Some may wonder why God might have chosen the historical sequence of intercessors first, prophets second and apostles third. This can be explained by highlighting the principal function of each of the three offices. The task of intercessors, for example, is to stand in the gap between the visible world and the invisible world. God gives them a supernatural ability to clear the pathway between heaven and Earth. When they succeed in removing the roadblocks that the enemy has erected, God's voice can be heard much more clearly by those of us on Earth. The members of the Body of Christ most gifted to hear the voice of the Lord are the prophets. Let me repeat: "Surely the Lord GOD does nothing, unless He reveals His secret to His servants the prophets" (Amos 3:7). The prophets clearly hear the voice of God. However, prophets typically are not gifted to know how to *apply* it to a given concrete situation. Implementing the will of God, generally speaking, is the task of apostles, those who are specially equipped to set things in order (see Titus 1:5).

Once all of this came into place in 2001, I began to feel comfortable using the label "Second Apostolic Age." The First Apostolic Age would have characterized the first couple of centuries of the Church. We are left then with a period of 1,800 years when the biblical government of the Church was not explicitly in its proper place. Despite this, the Church did continue to grow through the centuries in fulfillment of Jesus' proclamation that He would build His Church and that the very gates of Hades would not be able to stop it (see Matt. 16:18). I am excited because I am convinced that the best years for the expansion of the kingdom of God here on Earth lie ahead.

A Significant Movement

Even though the New Apostolic Reformation is a relatively recent development, it is not an insignificant part of world Christianity.

David B. Barrett, one of the most accomplished statisticians of the Christian church, has divided world Christianity into six "megablocs." Roman Catholics compose the largest megabloc, but of the five non-Catholic megablocs, the one embracing the New Apostolic Reformation (Barrett uses the terms "Independent," "Postdenominational" and "Neo-Apostolic") is the largest. It is larger, for example, than Anglicans, Orthodox, Protestants and Marginals (Mormons, Jehovah's Witnesses, etc.).[2]

Not only do the new apostolic churches compose the world's largest non-Catholic megabloc, but the number of churches also are currently growing much faster than that of all the other five megablocs combined. In his massive research report *World Christian Trends, AD 30-AD 2200*, David B. Barrett finds that the churches of what I call the Second Apostolic Age have increased in number by 323 percent between 1970 and 2000, compared to a 65-percent increase of all other churches over the same 30 years.[3]

Furthermore, these churches are so radically different from traditional churches that Barrett is able to list no fewer than 280 dichotomies between what he calls "two worldwide church lifestyles."[4] The title of the section in which he analyzes churches of the New Apostolic Reformation is quite revealing: "The Shift to Postdenominationalism in Church Lifestyles Worldwide." Barrett regards this phenomenon as "the latest in a long line of major historical realignments within global Christianity."[5]

Interestingly enough, among all six of Barrett's megablocs, the New Apostolic Reformation is the only one currently growing faster than Islam.

A NEW WINESKIN

I have already mentioned that the New Apostolic Reformation is bringing radical change to the Church. Let's look at what happens during changes like this. Take, for example, one of the most radical changes that we find in the Bible—the change from the Old Covenant to the New Covenant.

One of the ways that Jesus described this change was that God was moving His people from an old wineskin to a new wineskin.

At one point in Jesus' ministry, the disciples of John the Baptist, who were in a bad mood, approached Jesus (see Matt. 9:14-17). They were upset (to read between the lines) because they were so hungry. John had been making them fast all the time. But here were Jesus' disciples eating, drinking and enjoying themselves. They asked Jesus to help them understand how such a thing could be.

After comparing Himself and His disciples with a bridegroom and the friends of the bridegroom and using an analogy of patches on unshrunk cloth, Jesus talked to them about old wineskins and new wineskins.

Obviously, John the Baptist and his disciples were seen as the old wineskin. In fact, John was the last great representative of the Old Covenant. Jesus once said that the least in the kingdom of God was greater than John the Baptist (see Matt. 11:11), comparing the New Covenant with the Old Covenant. Jesus and His disciples were the first representatives of the New Covenant—the new wineskin.

Jesus said, "[People do not] put new wine into old wineskins, or else the wineskins break, the wine is spilled, and the wineskins are ruined. But they put new wine into new wineskins, and both are preserved" (Matt. 9:17). Apparently, the reason God does not pour His new wine into an old wineskin is due to His mercy. He loves the old wineskin and He does not want to ruin it. Every old wineskin was, at one point in time, a new wineskin. The Old Covenant once contained God's new wine. Jesus loved John the Baptist. He said that no man had been born of woman greater than John (see Matt.11:11). God does not condemn the old wineskin, but at the same time He will not pour His new wine into it. Its season has passed.

TODAY WE HAVE ENTERED ANOTHER NEW WINESKIN, THE SECOND APOSTOLIC AGE.

Let's also keep in mind that old wine is often more desirable than new wine. As Luke records this parable, he adds something not found in Matthew's account: "And no one, having drunk old wine, immediately desires new; for he says, 'The old is better'" (Luke 5:39). If wine connoisseurs, in the days when wine was stored in skins, went into a wine cellar and had the choice between wine in old wineskins and wine in new wineskins, they would almost invariably choose the old. What God did in the past was good—so good that it is understandable that some might not want new wine at all. However, God has chosen to pour out new wine. We must trust that for those who are moving into the Second Apostolic Age, it is more desirable than the old wine.

Trace the history of the Church and you will see that God has created new wineskin after new wineskin for His Church. Today we have entered another new wineskin, which I call the Second Apostolic Age. Radical changes in the way we do church are not around the corner; they are already here with us.

Are you ready?

POWERFUL RESISTANCE

Some will say no to that question, which is understandable. They are not ready for change because they know that change won't be easy. The change from an old wineskin to a new wineskin inevitably meets powerful resistance. This resistance does not come from the *anointed* leaders of the old wineskin, but from the *unanointed* leaders of the old wineskin.

John the Baptist is an excellent example of an anointed old-wineskin leader. Nicodemus, Gamaliel and others could be mentioned as well. John said things like, "He who is coming after me is mightier than I, whose sandals I am not worthy to carry" (Matt. 3:11). And again,

> I said, "I am not the Christ," but, "I have been sent before Him."
> He who has the bride is the bridegroom; but the friend of the
> bridegroom, who stands and hears him, rejoices greatly because
> of the bridegroom's voice. . . . He must increase, but I must
> decrease (John 3:28-30).

Other prominent leaders of the Old Covenant were the Pharisees, and they were clearly *unanointed* leaders. They were the opposite of John the Baptist. Instead of acclaiming and blessing God's new wineskin, they resisted it. Since they were powerful enough to get their way politically, they attempted to obliterate the new wineskin by killing Jesus.

SATAN'S DEVICES

What was going on behind the pernicious attack of the Pharisees? I am convinced that it should be attributed to nothing less than the activity of a demonic force. If it is and if it can be seen as a predictable reaction from old-wineskin leaders toward a new wineskin, we would do well to understand it as best as we can. Paul tells us that Satan will take advantage of us if we remain ignorant of his devices (see 2 Cor. 2:11), so let's not be ignorant of this particular device of Satan.

Two contrasting references in the book of Daniel will help us. In Daniel 2 we are told that God "changes the times and the seasons" (v. 21). God steadily moves forward. Part of His very nature is not to be static but to be fluid. In other words, God continually provides new wineskins for the new wine that He desires to pour out for His people.

However, Satan does not like this, to say the least. His desire is to change God's times and seasons back to where they were. For example, in Daniel 7 we meet the fourth beast, obviously a representative of Satan. What does he do? "He shall speak pompous words against the Most High, shall *persecute* the saints of the Most High, and shall intend to change times and law" (v. 25, emphasis added).

What devices does Satan use to do this? The Hebrew word translated as "persecute" is *belaw*, meaning "to wear out."[6] It is interesting that this wearing out is used in the Bible only in a mental sense. If we take it literally, then, it would mean that Satan tries to prevent God's new times and seasons from coming by sending evil demonic spirits to work particularly on our minds. If they are successful, we begin to think wrongly about the new wineskins that God desires to develop.

THE CORPORATE SPIRIT OF RELIGION

Can we identify this demonic spirit or spirits? I think we can. My hypothesis is that its functional name would be the corporate spirit of religion.

Here is a concise definition of the spirit of religion: The spirit of religion is an agent of Satan assigned to prevent change and maintain the status quo by using religious devices.

I'm using the term "religion" in the common sense of the word, namely beliefs and activities involved in relating to superhuman or supernatural beings or forces.

Knowing what we do about the invisible world of darkness, we can surmise certain things. For example, there certainly must be many spirits of religion, not just one. Consequently, our term "the spirit of religion" should be understood as a generic term, embracing however many of these demons there might actually be.

THE SPIRIT OF RELIGION IS AN AGENT OF SATAN ASSIGNED TO PREVENT CHANGE AND MAINTAIN THE STATUS QUO BY USING RELIGIOUS DEVICES.

THE LUCIFERIAN DEPARTMENT OF RELIGION

Now I am going to use my imagination a bit in order to illustrate the nature of Satan's subversive work. Let's imagine that Satan's kingdom has a Luciferian Department of Religion. If it does, there could well be two divisions: the Division of Non-Christian Religions and the Division of Christendom.

The issue for the spirit, or principality, controlling the Division of Non-Christian Religions is to whom an individual or a group gives allegiance. Keep in mind that the spirit of religion always attempts to preserve the status quo. In this case, it uses religion to keep people from switching their allegiance to Jesus Christ. It devises strategies to keep Moroccans committed to Allah or the Japanese to the Sun Goddess or the Thai to Buddha or the Aymaras of the Andes to Inti, just to choose a few examples.

Let's also assume that there are at least two offices in the Division of Christendom. The first could be the Office of Personal Religious Security. This would primarily target individuals, and the central issues for it are either salvation or fullness. The spirit of religion's first strategy here is to promote the idea that belonging to a Christian church or doing religious things brings salvation. It succeeds when it, for example, can persuade Catholics to think that they can be saved by lighting candles to Mary, or Baptists that they can be saved by going to church every Sunday and carrying a Bible, or Lutherans that they are saved if they have been baptized and confirmed.

If the personal spirit of religion cannot prevent an individual from believing in Christ and being saved, it then tries to keep that believer from growing in relationship with God. It does not allow believers to move on to the infilling of the Holy Spirit or to freedom in Christ or to the fulfillment of God's destiny for their lives. Paul specifically warns that the devil, by his craftiness, can corrupt *minds* and can keep them from "the simplicity that is in Christ" (2 Cor. 11:3).

The second Christendom-related office could be the Office of Corporate Church Structure. Here the spirit of religion targets the religious power brokers, those who determine the destiny of whole organizations, such as denominations. The central issue is God's new times and seasons. The demonic strategy is to preserve the status quo by getting people to adhere to the traditions of the elders.

This corporate spirit of religion is a major force of the enemy to discourage people from moving into the new wineskin of the Second Apostolic Age. It is not a personal spirit of religion, such as a spirit of rejection or a spirit of trauma or a spirit of lust, which invades individuals and which needs to be cast out of its victims. Rather, the assignment of the corporate spirit of religion is collective. It works on groups. It casts a spell over the leaders of whole segments of God's people. This, for example, is reflected in Galatians 3:1 (emphasis added): "O foolish Galatians! Who has *bewitched* you that you should not obey the truth?" The Galatians were under the spell of the corporate spirit of religion. They hesitated to move into God's new times and seasons for them.

The corporate spirit of religion does not speak out loud, write on walls, bring fire down from heaven or make furniture float through the air. Rather it quietly aims for human minds, as the Hebrew word "belaw" implies. Consequently, men and women who are in positions of influence in religious structures, presumably serving God, will unconsciously allow themselves to be manipulated mentally by evil spirits. By this I do not mean that they are demon possessed, but I do mean that demons are influencing their thoughts. They are under a spell. They unknowingly and unintentionally join the ranks of the unanointed leaders of old wineskins.

Jesus tells us, not once but seven times, in the book of Revelation, "He who has an ear, let him hear what the Spirit says [present tense] to the churches" (Rev. 2:7, et al). The spirit of religion wants to wear us out mentally (belaw) so that we do not hear. It causes religious leaders to concentrate not on what the Spirit is saying (present tense), but on what the Spirit said (past tense) in a former season. In other words, this spirit causes a desire in them to preserve the status quo. More than that, religious leaders like the Pharisees think that preserving the status quo is the will of God.

FEAR OF CHANGE

A major reason that many old-wineskin leaders do not want to hear some of the new things that the Spirit is saying to the churches is fear. They are fearful because change threatens them and it pulls them out of their comfort zones. When insecure people face change, they typically ask the question, "What am I going to lose?" This is too bad; they should be asking, "What is the kingdom of God going to gain?"

A vivid example of this is Peter, for whom one day began as the best of days but ended up the worst of days. When Jesus asked His disciples who they thought He was, Peter said, "You are the Christ, the Son of the living God" (Matt. 16:16). Jesus highly commended him with the words,

"Blessed are you, Simon Bar-Jonah, for flesh and blood has not revealed this to you, but My Father who is in heaven" (v. 17). This started off as a good day.

However, Jesus then told them for the first time that soon He would suffer, die and rise again and, after that, leave the disciples on their own. He was announcing a new time and season. Peter did not like this. He said, "Far be it from You, Lord; this shall not happen to You" (v. 22). Peter wanted to preserve the status quo. Where did Peter get this idea? Evidently it came from a superhuman source originating in the world of darkness, because Jesus immediately said to Peter, "Get behind Me, Satan!" (v. 23). It ended up as a bad day for Peter.

This seems to be a clear example of how the corporate spirit of religion works. This was not a demon that was going to make Peter lose his salvation, send him to an insane asylum or get him in bed with a harlot. It was not a personal spirit of religion that dominated his spiritual life. It was undoubtedly a high-ranking principality that prevented his mind from recognizing that the proposed change in times and seasons was from God.

This is exactly the mind-set that we frequently observe in leaders of today's old religious wineskins who find ways to object to the changes that God is bringing in the Second Apostolic Age. They are good people, as good as Peter was, but they nevertheless are yielding to the corporate spirit of religion, that principality of darkness who wants them to preserve the status quo.

What are these changes associated with the Second Apostolic Age? In the balance of this book, I will highlight a number of them.

CHAPTER TWO

FROM DENOMINATIONAL GOVERNMENT TO APOSTOLIC GOVERNMENT

MOST OF US IN CHRISTIAN LEADERSHIP THESE DAYS HAVE BEEN ASSOCIATED WITH PROTESTANT DENOMINATIONS FOR VARYING LENGTHS OF TIME. WE ACTUALLY HAD FEW OTHER OPTIONS SINCE DENOMINATIONS WERE, TO USE JESUS' TERM, THE WINESKIN OF CHOICE TO PROVIDE STRUCTURE TO THE CHRISTIAN MOVEMENT FOR SOME 300 YEARS.

NEW WINESKINS

The wineskin that preceded denominations was state churches. State churches were based on a pervasive concept of territorialism. Society, during much of history, presumed that church and state were supposed to be one. The religion of the prince or king of a territory automatically was the religion of all the citizens of the territory dominated by the ruler. This was not only true of the Roman Catholic and Eastern Orthodox churches, but religious territorialism was also carried over by the Reformers. This is how Sweden, for example, converted from Catholicism to Lutheranism in virtually one day by King Gustavus Vasa in 1527. This is how King Henry VIII decided that England should no longer be Catholic and decreed the establishment of the Church of England, which would no longer report to the Pope in Rome.

Keep in mind that, beginning with the Protestant Reformation, the non-Roman state churches were the new wineskin. However, the major changes from the old wineskin at that time were mostly theological versus structural. The translation of the Bible from Latin to the vernacular, combined with the doctrine of the priesthood of all believers, significantly changed the nature of church life. It is true that in some territories free churches existed separate from the state, but they were at best tolerated, not respected, and at worst persecuted by society as a whole.

When state churches became an old wineskin, the new wineskin that emerged, namely denominations, was initially formed in America.[1] Immigrants from England, Germany, Sweden, Scotland, the Netherlands and other countries found themselves in a territory containing a variety of religions. They could maintain their own faith within a territory as long as they alone occupied a particular section of that territory, but they found that they could not maintain religious territoriality for long. Furthermore, the constitution for the new American republic specifically prohibited the government from establishing a state church. (As an aside, it is noteworthy to mention that this clause had nothing to do with an attempt to separate religion from government, as some of today's liberal-minded activists would like us to believe.)

Also, as European state churches began to send missionaries to other parts of the world, the pattern of state churches could not be maintained there. Often the rulers of the nations on the mission field were not Christians. And frequently several state churches would plant churches in the same foreign territory.

I have explained this in order to help us keep in mind that denominations were, at one point in history, new wineskins. God was pouring His new wine into them, and He used the denominational structure in an extraordinary way to spread the gospel around the world. Even though denominations have now become old wineskins, seeing the broad picture helps all of us keep them in high respect, just as Jesus respected John the Baptist, who represented the old wineskin of His day.

THE RISE OF DEMOCRATIC CHURCH GOVERNMENT

Inherent in the American social process, in which denominations were formed, was the political ideal of democracy. Consequently, most denominations were established on the premise that democratic rule needed to be incorporated into their legal structure. It is important to realize that the introduction of democracy into church government came largely from the culture of the time rather than from biblical exegesis. As we soon shall see, this becomes very significant in the transition from the wineskin of denominations to the current new wineskin of apostolic government.

Ironically, most denominations were originally founded by apostles, even though the term itself was seldom used. Few would doubt that Martin Luther (Lutheran), John Knox (Presbyterian), John Wesley (Methodist), Menno Simons (Mennonite), William Booth (Salvation Army), George Fox (Quaker), Phineas Bresee (Nazarene), Alexander Campbell (Christian Church/Church of Christ), Aimee Semple McPherson (Foursquare) and many others like them were, in fact, apostles. Their apostolic leadership, however, could not be carried over to future generations. Through the process of routinization of charisma, first analyzed by pioneer sociologist Max Weber, democratic structures almost invariably took shape in the second generation or soon thereafter. The final authority of denominational government shifted inevitably from an *individual* to a *group*.

Interestingly enough, group authority even emerged in denominations that had adopted an episcopal, or bishop-led, government. While bishops and archbishops had more top-down power in Episcopal churches than district superintendents had in Nazarene churches, for example, they still did not have the power to choose their own successors. Denominational constitutions and bylaws typically assigned this responsibility to a group. Individual leaders were kept in line with denominational values through varying systems of legal checks and balances.

A Doctrine of Democratic Government

In the last chapter I argued that, as new wineskins eventually become old wineskins, the corporate spirit of religion will commonly attempt to lodge itself among the old-wineskin power brokers. This turns out to be such a quiet, behind-the-scenes, long-term process that it is almost impossible for insiders to perceive the subtle demonic activity in their midst. The corporate spirit of religion targets its most decisive work on the minds of leaders, individually and collectively. Its goal is to preserve the status quo of the old wineskin, not allowing the wineskin to move into God's new times and seasons.

The corporate spirit of religion works the same today as it did when it caused the Pharisees to equate the traditions of the elders with the sovereign will of God. They asked Jesus, "Why do Your disciples transgress the traditions of the elders?" (Matt. 15:2). In response, Jesus used harsh language. He accused them of "teaching as doctrines the commandments of men" (Matt. 15:9). Jesus also said, "You have made the commandment of God of no effect by your tradition" (Matt. 15:6). To say the least, the Pharisees clearly were not hearing what the Spirit was then saying to the "churches" (see Rev. 2:7).

THE CORPORATE SPIRIT OF RELIGION TARGETS ITS MOST DECISIVE WORK ON THE MINDS OF LEADERS, INDIVIDUALLY AND COLLECTIVELY.

One of the traditions of the elders, so to speak, in denominations is that democratic rule has over time become a de facto doctrine. A major threat to the status quo, therefore, would be to allow the introduction of apostles who do not see themselves as subject to democratic processes. This is to say nothing of prophets, who have developed a frightening reputation of shaking up the status quo wherever the prophets might be found. It should come as no surprise, then, that the mind-set of denominational leaders would oppose whatever they might perceive to be a threat to the doctrine of democratic ecclesiastical government.

It was not until recently that, at least in the United States, denominational leaders began to perceive that threat. As I have mentioned, I believe that the year 2001 might be seen as the time that a critical mass for the Second Apostolic Age had first been set into place. Even so, many denominational leaders still are unaware of contemporary apostles. For example, at this writing I have not yet seen the subject discussed in

Christianity Today magazine, the voice of the evangelical wing of the church. However, since a large segment of the New Apostolic Reformation has emerged from American independent charismatics, both charismatics and classical Pentecostals are well aware of contemporary apostles by now. Therefore, they have been discussed to some extent in *Charisma* magazine, the charismatic counterpart of *Christianity Today*.

THE NEWEST OLD WINESKINS

Consider this axiom: The strongest opposition to a new wineskin will, more than likely, come from representatives of the most recent old wineskin. This has actually been happening. Take, for example, one of the most dramatic apostolic events to date: the simultaneous public commissioning of 12 apostles, each leading a different network, before a stadium crowd of 30,000 believers in Guatemala City in 2000. As soon as they heard that this was being planned, some of the chief Guatemalan Pentecostal leaders, not too long ago pioneers of their own new wineskin, launched a massive media attack that denounced the idea that these could be legitimate apostles, nearly succeeding in their goal of having the commissioning service cancelled.

In the United States, the most vocal and concerted attack against the idea of there being legitimate apostles and prophets in the Church today has come from the Assemblies of God, headquartered in Springfield, Missouri. Because it is important in a book like this to familiarize ourselves with the arguments used against apostles, I will quote Assemblies of God leaders from time to time. I would not want this to lead to the conclusion that I am intentionally singling out the Assemblies of God, but the fact is that the most explicit arguments currently in print originate from them. If the Presbyterians, the Christian Reformed Church, the Free Methodists, the Congregationalists or other denominations had published official statements on the subject, I would have quoted from them as well, but to my knowledge they have not.

ISSUES OF THE DEBATE

American Assemblies of God leaders became aware that there might be apostles today when a movement called the Latter Rain, which I mentioned in the previous chapter, took shape within classical Pentecostalism in the 1940s. The Latter Rain embraced the ministry of apostles and prophets. Not surprisingly, they were condemned by their first cousins, so to speak, the Assemblies of God, because they threatened the status quo, particularly the doctrine of democracy. The Assemblies of God General Council published an official denominational white paper in 1949 stating: "The teaching that the Church is built on the foundation of present-day apostles and prophets [is] erroneous."[2] The criticism was so severe that the Latter Rain never flourished, as many expected it would.

However, the apostolic movement surfaced again when the New Apostolic Reformation began to take shape in the 1990s. True to form, the American Assemblies of God published another denominational white paper in 2000, stating that the "teaching that present-day offices of apostles and prophets should govern church ministry" is "a departure from Scripture and a deviant teaching."[3] In 2001, their general secretary, George Wood, circulated a theological essay, "Apostleship in the Church Today," arguing his view that the New Testament's references to apostles and prophets referred to the role of these offices in the first century or two as the Bible was being written and compiled but that there are no longer New Testament-type apostles and prophets today.

This point of view provoked an Australian Assemblies of God leader, David Cartledge, to refer to the American Assemblies of God as "Pentecostal Cessationists."[4] He pointed out the irony that Pentecostals themselves, who for the better part of the twentieth century had argued strongly—against evangelical cessationists—that *all* of the gifts of the Holy Spirit were in effect today, were now rejecting two offices derived expressly from the gifts of the Spirit. They were, of course, the two offices perceived as the most threatening to the doctrine of democratic church government.

THE ISSUE OF AUTHORITY

The reason why democratic denominations would feel so threatened by apostolic government is no mystery. The most radical change brought about by the new wineskin is this: the amount of spiritual authority delegated by the Holy Spirit to individuals. The two operative words in this statement are "authority" and "individuals."

In the old wineskin, authority invariably resided in groups. That is why terms such as "deacon boards," "sessions," "vestries," "consistories," "congregational meetings," "presbyteries," "synods," "district councils," "general assemblies," "mission boards," "plurality of elders," "cabinets," "study commissions," "general councils," "executive committees" and the like have become common currency among denominational churches. The underlying message is that individuals should not be entrusted with the kind of decision making that might affect a whole church body.

Conversely, the principal characteristic that distinguishes apostles from other members of the Body of Christ is individual authority. Paul asserted this when he told the Corinthians that he could boast about the authority that he had received from the Lord (see 2 Cor. 10:8). At the Council of Jerusalem, James said to the other apostles, "Listen to *me*" (Acts 15:13, emphasis added) and later "Therefore *I* judge" (Acts 15:19, emphasis added). John said, "If anyone comes to you and does not bring this doctrine, do not receive him into your house nor greet him" (2 John 10). Paul said, "If anyone does not obey our word in this epistle, note that person and do not keep company with him, that he may be ashamed" (2 Thess. 3:14). It goes without saying that these are extremely authoritative statements.

One of the more obvious implications of this is that in apostolic meetings, such as the Jerusalem Council, decisions are not made by voting. I was amused by some recent comments by the respected Lutheran scholar and historian, Martin Marty. Marty, who identifies himself as a supporter of denominations, expresses his discomfort with denominational assemblies and says that new models and manners for denominational assemblies are called for. His suggestion: "My solution to the problem is simple: Don't let the people vote. What leads up to voting is what messes everything up."[5]

Here is Marty's description of what commonly happens in an old-wineskin denominational annual meeting:

> Participants typically arrive on Sunday evening full of joy, hugging each other. A triumphant opening ceremony follows. On Monday people cheer at reports, however mixed the news. But on Tuesday committees begin their reports, and the clouds roll in. Wednesday, participants debate the committees' recommendations. Thursday they vote. Friday they all go home mad, even the winners, who know their victories are temporary.[6]

I think that the way James ran the Council of Jerusalem is a better system. But it takes an apostle to make it happen.

IT IS CURIOUS THAT MANY CHRISTIAN LEADERS WHO ARE COMFORTABLE WITH THE OFFICES OF EVANGELIST AND PASTOR AND TEACHER IMAGINE THAT APOSTLES AND PROPHETS SHOULD BE RELEGATED TO BYGONE DAYS.

PROOF TEXTS FOR APOSTOLIC AUTHORITY

Those who feel uncomfortable with apostolic authority would do well to reexamine four clear biblical proof texts.

The first is Ephesians 4:11: "And [Jesus] Himself gave some to be apostles, some prophets, some evangelists, and some pastors and teachers." It is curious that many Christian leaders who are comfortable with the offices of evangelist and pastor and teacher imagine that the two others mentioned in the same sentence, apostles and prophets, should be relegated to bygone days.

The second is Ephesians 2:20: "[The household of God is] built on the foundation of the apostles and prophets, Jesus Christ Himself being the chief cornerstone." Some would argue that these apostles and prophets completed their task of laying the foundation of the Church in the first century or two. Such is a form of cessationism.

The third is 1 Corinthians 12:28: "And God has appointed these in the church: first apostles, second prophets, third teachers, after that miracles, then gifts of healings, helps, administrations, varieties of tongues." Most of those who contend that apostles and prophets are not for today would not want to go on to say that other gifts such as teachers, miracles, healings, helps, administrations, and tongues are not for today either. It seems a bit inconsistent.

However, the clearest Scripture related to the duration of the offices of apostle and prophet comes right after the list of apostles, prophets, evangelists, pastors and teachers in Ephesians 4:11. The Bible goes on to say that the purpose of these five offices is to equip "the saints for the work of ministry" (Eph. 4:12). How long will they be needed? "Till we all come to the unity of the faith and of the knowledge of the Son of God, to a perfect man, to the measure of the stature of the fullness of Christ" (Eph. 4:13). Unless someone believes that we have actually reached that point, it is difficult to suppose that we no longer need the ministry of apostles and prophets.

CHURCH GOVERNMENT

I have spent quite a bit of time attempting to clarify the contrast between the concepts of denominational church government and apostolic church government. To fill in the picture, it would be good to take a brief look at how this is playing out in real church life as a growing number of leaders are now moving into the new wineskin of the Second Apostolic Age.

The authority that the Holy Spirit is delegating to individuals in this new wineskin plays out in two arenas: on the local church level in the role of the pastor and on the translocal level in the role of apostle.

The Local Church Level

On the local church level, there are five general assumptions concerning the role of the pastor in the old denominational wineskins:

1. Pastors are employees of the church.
2. Pastors can come and go. The average pastoral tenure among Southern Baptists, for example, is less than 3 years.
3. Pastors are enablers. Their responsibility is to implement the vision of the congregation.
4. Pastors are the "medicine men" of the church rather than the "tribal chiefs." They are expected to do religious things but not to lead.
5. Pastors are subject to performance reviews. They can be fired at will.

In contrast, apostolic churches make a different set of assumptions concerning the local church pastor:

1. Pastors—not the congregations—cast the vision.
2. Pastors major in leadership and minor in management.
3. Pastors make top-drawer policy decisions and delegate the rest.
4. Pastors build a solid management team of both elders and staff. Pastors are not subject to the authority of this team, but the team serves at the pleasure of the pastors. Staff members are employees of their pastor, not of the church.
5. Pastors are called for life.
6. Pastors choose their successors.

The Translocal Level

Denominational leadership has largely been in the hands of administrators, commonly referred to as denominational executives. Most of them actually began their ministerial careers as pastors. In many cases, the career switch from local church pastor to translocal denominational executive posts has been interpreted by their superiors, as well as by most of their peers, as a promotion. It is true that, by and large, such promotions were ordinarily based on the perception that these individuals also had gifts of leadership and/or administration, but their primary identity often remained as pastors. A bishop, a district superintendent or a synod president would frequently describe his or her role as a pastor to pastors. In addresses to their constituency at denominational gatherings, more often than not they would make occasional reference to their experience as a local church pastor. Most of them chose to operate from a pastoral mind-set.

Denominational constitutions and bylaws ordinarily created administrative positions that carried authority over the churches in a given territory. Pastors, then, were made accountable to leaders to whom they were expected to relate simply because of the leader's legal position in the bureaucracy. In some denominations, the leader was appointed from the top down and the pastors had no say in the matter. However, even in denominations in which translocal leaders were elected, the pastors who did not happen to vote with the majority typically found themselves in a situation that was not of their making.

Translocal apostolic leadership is quite different. It stands or falls, not on an ecclesiastical position, but on personal relationships. Apostolic networks replace denominations. Local churches are autonomous, and as I have said, the pastors are the leaders of the congregations. They decide whether or not to place themselves under the "spiritual covering" of a translocal apostle. This means that they enter into a mutual personal agreement that the apostle will assume spiritual authority over the pastor, speak into the pastor's life, deal with ministry issues that require outside assistance, encourage the pastor and serve as a spiritual father. In turn, the pastor contributes financially to the salary and expenses of the apostle. Note that this agreement is sustained only so long as the personal relationship remains positive.

Since the affiliation with an apostle and with his or her apostolic network begins voluntarily, pastors can also leave voluntarily. However, current practice shows that, with the exception of cases in which, for one reason or another, the apostle violates personal and professional integrity, this rarely happens. Why? It is because apostolically oriented pastors feel that the apostle adds value to their life and ministry. They are convinced that they would not be able to reach their full destiny in serving God apart from the spiritual covering of the apostle. This allows them not only to contribute financially to the apostle's ministry but also to be cheerful givers.

PASTORS AND APOSTLES ARE AS DIFFERENT FROM EACH OTHER AS HANDS ARE DIFFERENT FROM EYES.

PASTORAL MIND-SET VERSUS APOSTOLIC MIND-SET

One interesting way to look at the transition from denominational government to apostolic government is to contrast what could be called a pastoral mind-set with an apostolic mind-set. I have explained how denominational executives tend to see themselves in a pastoral role, as pastors to pastors. This does not generally hold true with apostles.

By saying this, I do not mean to imply that apostles are by any stretch of the imagination more important in God's design for the Body of Christ than pastors. That would be like the eye saying to the hand, "I have no need of you" (1 Cor. 12:21). The Church could not operate without pastors. I do mean, however, that pastors and apostles are as different from each other as hands are different from eyes. Each has its essential place in the Body. The pastoral mind-set is absolutely necessary for the health of the local congregation. But when it comes to the area of *translo-*

cal government, we are seeing a shift from the *pastoral* mind-set of the old wineskin to the *apostolic* mind-set characteristic of the new wineskin.

One of our outstanding contemporary apostles, Jim Hodges of Federation of Ministers and Churches, has given considerable thought to this difference, and with his permission, I will borrow several of his conclusions.

- The pastoral mind-set focuses primarily on individual believers, the "sheep," as it should. The apostolic mind-set focuses on the corporate vision and outreach of the local church.
- The pastoral mind-set wants to take the congregation, the "flock," to its next level of service to God. The apostolic mind-set goes beyond the congregation and targets city and regional transformation.
- The pastoral mind-set attempts to maintain harmony, balance, peace and stability. The apostolic mind-set pushes out to the frontiers of the mission of God with all the risks involved in aggressive warfare.
- The pastoral mind-set regards the church as the family of God. Socialization becomes important. The apostolic mind-set regards the church as the army of God. Effective strategy becomes important. Pastors want their people in the bedroom (intimacy with God), while apostles want them on the battlefield (warfare against the devil).
- Pastors are comfortable with and connect better with teachers. Apostles, on the other hand, are more comfortable with and connect better with prophets.
- The pastoral mind-set avoids controversy so that everything remains settled. The apostolic mind-set welcomes and confronts controversy with the goal of resolution.[7]

A NEW APOSTOLIC DIRECTION

It would not be fair to suppose that the old wineskin is all pastoral while the new wineskin is all apostolic. There is, of course, considerable blending and overlapping between the two. However, those who wish to understand the Second Apostolic Age as thoroughly as possible can safely regard the move from the pastoral mind-set to the apostolic mind-set as an unmistakable current trend in church government.

CHAPTER THREE

FROM INTERNAL REFORM TO APOSTOLIC RENEWAL

IN 1959, DENNIS BENNETT, WHO WAS SERVING AS AN EPISCOPAL PRIEST IN VAN NUYS, CALIFORNIA, EXPERIENCED A PERSONAL TOUCH FROM THE HOLY SPIRIT. AMONG OTHER THINGS, HE RECEIVED THE GIFT OF SPEAKING IN TONGUES. BY THE FOLLOWING YEAR, THE NEWS HAD BEGUN TO SPREAD ACROSS THE COUNTRY, AND MANY OTHER BELIEVERS STARTED SEEKING OUT DENNIS BENNETT TO HELP THEM ENTER INTO A SIMILAR EXPERIENCE OF PERSONAL SPIRITUAL RENEWAL.

Thus began the contemporary renewal movement within established Christian church bodies in the United States. I do not wish to ignore the fact that the renewal movement also had significant international ripple effects; however, the forms the renewal has taken have varied considerably from place to place around the world. In this chapter I will limit my comments primarily to what I have seen happening in the United States.

TWO BRANCHES OF RENEWAL

Actually, two prominent branches of the renewal movement developed over the last four decades of the twentieth century. The one traced to Dennis Bennett emphasized speaking in tongues and practicing other charismatic gifts, and consequently it became known as the charismatic renewal. The other focused on conservative evangelical theology, opposing growing trends toward liberalism in the mainline Protestant denominations. It has become known as evangelical renewal movements. The plural is appropriate because most denominations contained their own evangelical movements with their own history and leaders. In fact, the leaders of these conservative groups, unlike the leaders of the charismatic renewal, did not develop much contact with each other. It was only in 2002 that their first joint gathering was held.

Let's look first at the charismatic renewal.

THE CHARISMATIC RENEWAL

During the 1960s, the charismatic renewal grew, but not rapidly. However, as the 1970s began, excitement built and the rate of growth accelerated. By 1977, the Conference on Charismatic Renewal in the Christian Churches was held in Kansas City, pulling together more than 50,000 tongues-speakers from across the denominational spectrum.

As it has turned out, the Kansas City meeting is now seen as the apex of the charismatic renewal movement, even though its leaders at the time expected that it would only be the beginning of bigger things to come. In order to provide some structure for what was likely to come, the North American Renewal Service Committee was launched in 1986 under the leadership of Vinson Synan of the Pentecostal Holiness Church. National charismatic renewal conferences were then held in New Orleans (1987), Indianapolis (1990), Orlando (1995) and St. Louis (2000) with the hope of rekindling the intense spiritual fire seen in Kansas City. Disappointingly, attendance at these gatherings steadily declined.

Meanwhile, charismatic renewal movements had begun to take shape within most American denominations. It is true that some refused to open their doors to charismatic renewal of any kind, but they turned out to be the exceptions to the rule. The Roman Catholic Church entered the renewal stream through a revival at Duquesne University in 1967 and began to hold annual conferences for Spirit-filled Catholics. The peak came in 1973 when 30,000 Catholics attended.

THE GLENCOE GROUP

Most, if not all, of these denominational renewal movements coalesced under particular leaders, and the leaders then built relationships with each other. The Charismatic Concerns Committee (CCC) was formed and grew under the leadership of renewal activists such as Dennis Bennett, Larry Christenson, Kevin Ranaghan and, most notably, Vinson Synan of the Pentecostal Holiness Church. The CCC became an informal, invitation-only gathering of renewal leaders that met annually, more often than not at a Catholic retreat center in Glencoe, Missouri. It thus became known as the Glencoe Meeting or the Glencoe Group.

Although I had no denominational role, I was still regarded by some of the leaders as at least a marginal participant in the charismatic renewal movement because of the courses in signs and wonders that John Wimber and I had introduced to Fuller Theological Seminary, because of my charismatically-oriented adult Sunday School class in Lake Avenue Congregational Church and because I was a chief spokesperson for what I began calling the Third Wave. One consequence of this was that I was regularly invited to attend the Glencoe meetings. I did not feel that I should accept, however, because at the time I was advocating that those in the Third Wave should avoid, as much as possible, the label "charismatic."

By 2000, I was well into researching, teaching and writing on the subject of this book, the Second Apostolic Age. Vinson Synan felt that the Glencoe Group might be interested in hearing about apostolic ministry, so he asked me to share this at their annual meeting. What I looked forward to the most about attending their meeting was being introduced to these outstanding leaders of the charismatic renewal movement, many of them for the first time.

I was surprised by what I found in Glencoe.

INDEPENDENT CHARISMATIC CHURCHES

Before I explain this surprise, let me point out that the charismatic renewal actually had taken on two different forms. As I have said, the charismatic renewal movement, which began with Episcopalian Dennis Bennett in 1960, fed into the existing denominational structures. However, a number of local churches emphasizing the charismatic gifts began springing up across the country outside of the denominations. Small parts of this movement can be traced to the 1950s, but strong and highly visible momentum began to build around 1970. These churches became known as independent charismatic churches. It is notable that by the mid-1980s this group of churches had replaced denominational Pentecostals as the fastest-growing segment of American Christianity.[1]

The present generation of independent charismatics has now merged into what I am calling the New Apostolic Reformation. This is the group with which I identify. I have changed my membership from a Congregational church to a new apostolic church, and I no longer resist the label "charismatic."

The church leaders from across the nation with whom I now largely associate constitute what I would not hesitate to describe as the most upbeat, excited, positive, visionary and high-energy group imaginable. I attribute this largely to the dynamic activity of the Holy Spirit among them. When I first went to Glencoe, I expected to encounter more of the same. I was surprised, however, when I found something quite different.

A Vision Unfulfilled

The Glencoe leaders knew the filling of the Holy Spirit firsthand. They were among the heroes of the faith, the pioneers of the charismatic renewal movement. But by 2000, the glow had dimmed. Discouragement had set in. They seemed tired. The thought crossed my mind that I may be observing the end of the road.

Even though the individual members of the Glencoe Group had carved out reputations as highly respected Christian leaders, they were largely people whose life vision had never been fulfilled. In the 1960s and '70s, they had been bubbling with excitement about the ministry of the Holy Spirit. They had been personally renewed. Their worship was more intimate. Their prayer life was more powerful. They were moving in healing and prophecy and tongues. They were characterized by the fruit of the Spirit. They saw others receive the Holy Spirit as they prayed for them.

For the most part these individuals loved their denominations. They had a great desire to see spiritual renewal in the lives of their friends, in congregations, and in denominations as a whole. However, they fully realized that their denominations were in trouble. Beginning in 1965, virtually every one of the Protestant mainline denominations in the United States had begun losing members. The renewal leaders were convinced, however, that the power of the Holy Spirit could turn them around and make them vital once again. They fervently prayed that this would happen, and happen soon.

A solid core of men and women had dedicated their lives to the cause. They felt that God had called them to bring reform to their movements from the inside out. Their passion was to spread the exciting news of God's power. One of them, Francis MacNutt, said it as well as any: "Those were heady, exciting days when it seemed as if the entire Christian world would join the Pentecostal churches in rediscovering the essential value of the Baptism of the Spirit in renewing not only individual lives, but in renewing the entire body of Christ."[2]

Such a renewal, however, was not to be. By 2000, denial no longer could serve as a psychological prop. Not one of the American denominations had experienced the spiritual reformation that the leaders had been praying for. Charismatic renewal leaders looked back on 30 or 40 of the best years of their lives with remorse that their dreams had not come true. Yes, many individuals and some congregations had been spiritually transformed, but the structures at best had remained the same, and in some cases they had deteriorated even more.

The annual Glencoe Meeting helped. The leaders who had established close friendships enjoyed being with each other. They did their best to keep their spirits up. However, conversations in the corridors and around the tables were notably focused on the past rather than on fresh visions for the future.

What was going on? Why would such a large, biblically justified and seemingly God-inspired movement lose its steam?

It seems to me that there are two major reasons underlying this disappointment, both of which I introduced in the first chapter. One has to do with the principle of wineskins, and the second is related to the cunning tactics of the corporate spirit of religion.

DENOMINATIONS IN AMERICA

The history of Christianity in America has largely revolved around denominations. Denominations have been part of our nation's religious landscape since the coming of the earliest settlers. Our Constitution permanently institutionalized them. The doctrine of the separation of church and state was never intended by the Constitution's signers to separate God from government, as some attempt to interpret it today; it was simply a statement that the United States would never establish a state religion.

This was a major change from the situation in the European nations that gave us our early citizens. When the Dutch brought their Reformed churches and the British brought their Anglican churches and the Norwegians and Germans brought their Lutheran churches, just to list a few examples, their pastors in the New World were no longer employees of the government as they had been in the Old World. American denominations had become a new wineskin in the kingdom of God.

Not only was the concept of freestanding denominational structures a new wineskin, but also it opened the door for the addition of a constantly increasing number of additional denominations over the years, each of which might be seen as a new wineskin in itself. This provided an extraordinary vitality to American Christianity that European Christianity no longer enjoyed. Denominations became a standard fixture of church life in America for over 300 years. It could be said that the denominational wineskin exhibited notable endurance. As American religious history unfolded, many denominations became recipients of God's new wine.

A change is now occurring. As I detailed in chapter 2, the biblical government of the Church, with its foundation of apostles and prophets, has now come into place, at least in its initial phases. We have entered the New Apostolic Age. Denominational structures, for the most part, have now become old wineskins, and the process leading up to this change has been developing for some years.

NEW WINE IN OLD WINESKINS

Jesus teaches in Matthew 9 that God does not desire to pour His new wine into old wineskins because the wineskins will not be able to hold it. The wineskins will break, and both the wineskins and the wine will be lost.

While this insight is prevalent among leaders of the New Apostolic Reformation, it admittedly was not common knowledge during the time of the charismatic renewal. I do not believe that the thought even occurred to most of the charismatic renewal leaders that their efforts to introduce the dynamic of the person and work of the Holy Spirit into their denominations might have been, in fact, attempting to pour new wine into old wineskins. This observation is not in the least meant to imply blame. Hindsight always provides the clearest vision. But if Jesus' teaching in Matthew 9 is taken at face value, understanding the frustrations of the charismatic renewal movement becomes a bit easier.

ONE OF THE MAJOR ASSIGNMENTS THAT THE CORPORATE SPIRIT OF RELIGION HAS RECEIVED IS TO PREVENT THE CHURCH FROM BEING EVERYTHING IT IS SUPPOSED TO BE.

As I have said, one of the major assignments that the corporate spirit of religion apparently has received from the headquarters of darkness is to prevent the Church from being everything it is supposed to be. Blocking the penetration of the activity of the Holy Spirit into the structures of American denominations would clearly be one major way of fulfilling this purpose. I am amazed at the naked cleverness of the strategy that the enemy seemingly employed to accomplish his task.

For a starter, virtually every denomination opened its doors for the charismatic renewal movement. This was necessary to avoid potential division. Just a historical glimpse at how the holiness movement had separated from the Methodists and how the Pentecostal movement had separated from the holiness movement would be enough to alert the denominational leaders to take steps to try to avoid the recurrence of such a thing, and the best way to avoid it was not to reject the charismatic renewal outright.

The corporate spirit of religion had gone into full action. Others may explain it differently, but it seems to me that certain denominational executives must have received nothing less than supernatural wisdom to help them deal with an upstart movement that had the potential to seriously disturb the status quo. This supernatural wisdom, in my opinion, did not come from the realm of light but rather from the realm of darkness. However, it was so subtle that it actually appeared, in the minds of many, to be God's own design. Preserving the status quo was, in their minds, the will of God.

First, many denominational executives encouraged a season of dialogue. Then, when they knew that their constituency would no longer be taken by surprise, they began to affirm the charismatic renewal leaders. Some denominations accepted the renewal as part of their formal structure. Many of them chose to receive it as an adjunct to the denomination, although formally recognized. From time to time they would invite the renewal leaders to address their denominational assemblies both regionally and nationally. Renewal newsletters circulated freely throughout the denominations.

At the same time, however, many denominational leaders quietly but decisively constructed a glass ceiling over the renewal movement in their midst. While they had dutifully affirmed charismatic renewal, they also skillfully domesticated it. It was allowed to go so far, but no farther. Then, over time, they were able to lower the glass ceiling little by little. Few people, including many denominational executives, actually realized that this was happening. For many it was unintentional. Neverthelesss, the result was that the charismatic renewal movement steadily became less and less threatening to those who desired to preserve the denominational status quo.

Once the renewal movement had lost its initial strength and fervor, many denominations, to one degree or another, institutionalized it. It took its place as another entry on a long list of multiple activities that the denomination endorsed. But by then there was no longer any chance that it would ever become a high-priority denominational distinctive. The spirit of religion had accomplished its purpose.

EVANGELICAL RENEWAL MOVEMENTS

Let's shift our focus briefly from the charismatic renewal movement with its emphasis on the gifts of the Holy Spirit to the other form of general renewal, which stresses theological orthodoxy. Some sociologists of religion have labeled these theologically conservative groups with the technical term "evangelical renewal movements," or "ERMs" for short.[3]

As the prevalent theology of mainline American denominations became increasingly liberal during the twentieth century, ERMs began to take root across the spectrum. For the most part, they were regarded as "relatively silent fringe groups viewed as uninformed remnants of the past."[4] By the turn of the century, however, they seemed to gain new vitality and influence in many denominations. For example, the United Methodist Confessing Movement, an ERM, claimed more than 630,000 members and 1,400 churches in 2003.[5]

The vision of the ERM leaders, much like that of the early charismatic renewal leaders, is to renew their denominations theologically from within. Many of them hope that time will be on their side. They hope that the older liberal denominational executives will soon either retire or expire and that the younger renewal leaders, now more politically astute than previously, will take over.

All this is occurring despite the fact that many entrenched mainline denominational leaders, undoubtedly influenced by the spirit of religion, accuse the ERMs of being manipulated by a group of wealthy conservative conspirators. For example, Presbyterian Jack Rogers insists that the Presbyterian Confessing Church Movement, one of the strongest ERMs, "is not a grassroots movement" but "a tool of the conservative Presbyterian Lay Committee" designed to damage the denomination.[6]

Methodist professor Tex Sample says, "I really want to know why these right-wing foundations are financing . . . these kinds of wrongful attacks on the United Methodist Church."[7]

In Indianapolis in 2002, the ERM leaders from eight of the mainline denominations gathered for the first time to encourage one another. This Association for Church Renewal conference, although taking a different format, may be reminiscent of the Kansas City meeting of the charismatic renewal leaders in 1977. Time will tell. But meanwhile, it would not be surprising if the same spirit of religion went into action and caused the denominations to successfully domesticate these attempts to return to biblical theology. Like the majority of charismatic renewal leaders, most ERM proponents have determined not to abandon their denominations.

RELIGIOUS COVENANTS

Is there an alternative to attempting to pour new wine into old wineskins?

The answer to this rhetorical question is, Of course! Simply move into the new wineskins that God is providing.

I realize that this is an uncomfortable thought to many charismatics and evangelicals who are committed to staying in their denominations as agents of renewal. I would like to suggest, however, that the desire to stay, with all the good qualities of loyalty that it reflects, may be playing into the hands of the spirit of religion.

My hypothesis is that the spirit of religion is so deceptively skillful that it can subtly penetrate the very DNA of a religious structure. It casts a spell. Few denominational leaders would have the discernment to recognize its presence. If this is correct, then affiliation with some, but not all, denominations could automatically establish a covenant with the spirit of religion, which is embedded in its DNA. Because the spirit of religion is a demonic entity, the covenant, by definition, would be an ungodly covenant. Individuals, even those with the best intentions, who refuse to break this ungodly covenant would predictably experience unnecessary difficulty in fulfilling the destiny that God has mapped out for them.

Breaking the religious covenant is by no means easy. The spirit of religion has managed to develop attractions that keep members within the structure like magnets. Many leaders would not consider leaving their denomination because of one or more of these thoughts:

- *This is the church of my family. I would betray my family heritage.*
- *My friends are all here. They might turn against me if I left.*
- *The denomination holds my ordination credentials.*
- *The denomination owns our church facilities, and we would lose them.*
- *All my clergy colleagues, including my support group, are in the denomination.*
- *This is my employment. How could I support my family otherwise?*
- *My retirement funds are here, and I would forfeit them if I left.*
- *My religious affiliation has always been part of my personal self-identity.*
- *I must avoid the sin of rebellion and remain loyal.*

Despite the pain involved in leaving a denomination and breaking covenant with the corporate spirit of religion, an increasing number of renewal leaders are doing just that. They have given up on the notion of internal reform, and they are moving into a new wineskin of apostolic renewal.

These leaders, by and large, have not rejected their denominational roots. They have simply become more than dissatisfied with the spiritual and theological directions that have pulled their denominations away from the values of their apostolic founder or founders. In fact, they are convinced that they are more loyal to their denominational roots than are the denominational leaders now in control. They have become anxious to explore the possibility of new wineskins.

Nevertheless, large numbers of believers will maintain their long-standing denominational ties. Nothing in this book is to be construed as arguing that denominations are bad, even though they are obviously old wineskins. Old wine, generally speaking, is of the highest quality, but

God has chosen to give new wine. So those who choose to remain in the old wineskin should not be surprised if other believers and other groups are now the recipients of God's new wine.

AN INCREASING NUMBER OF RENEWAL LEADERS HAVE GIVEN UP ON THE NOTION OF INTERNAL REFORM AND ARE MOVING INTO A NEW WINESKIN OF APOSTOLIC RENEWAL.

ECUMENICITY VERSUS SEPARATION

The option of withdrawing from the hierarchical structure of the denomination would not have occurred to many of the first-generation renewal leaders. A major reason was that they, along with their peers, had been programmed with a pervasive view that unity was a supreme and inviolable Christian value. They were products of the ecumenical age, which in my opinion is another deceptive tactic of the spirit of religion. In the minds of many of them, whatever might tend to separate Christians from one another would clearly be contrary to God's will.

It might not have occurred to these first-generation leaders that most godly renewal movements of the past tended, in fact, to produce separation of Christians rather than ecumenicity. Although the renewal leaders did not desire to separate, separation became inevitable because, to use our terminology, God would not allow them to pour new wine into old wineskins. Lutherans need only to recall that their movement was initiated by Luther's separation from the Roman Catholic Church. One of the initial distinctives of Mennonites was Anabaptist separatism. John Wesley, the founder of the Methodist movement, eventually had to break from Anglicanism in order to receive God's full destiny for the movement. William Booth, in turn, had to leave the Methodist Church in order to start the Salvation Army. Presbyterians caught the initial fire of the Holy Spirit when John Knox rejected the Anglican Church. These are only a few examples among many.

It is also noteworthy that the most lasting results of the charismatic renewal movement were seen, not in the efforts to renew the existing denominations internally, but in the emergence of the independent charismatic churches, congregations that were planted outside of denominational structures and thus were beyond the reach of the corporate spirit of religion.

Today, members of a new generation of renewal leaders, while affirming biblical principles of Christian unity, are beginning to ask questions concerning its most viable forms. The vigorous efforts toward unity promoted by the ecumenical movement did not seem to bear positive fruit. If what we have done in the past has not worked, what then are the most viable options for the future?

Although the terminology I use in this book may not as yet have been adopted by some of the new generation of renewal leaders, I nevertheless suggest that the most viable option might be an *apostolic* view of unity as contrasted to a *pastoral* view of unity. What is the difference? Pastoral unity is mercy motivated, relational, politically correct, compromising, polite and peaceful. Apostolic unity is task oriented, visionary, aggressive, uncompromising, warlike and often abrasive. Renewal leaders like Martin Luther, John Knox and William Booth clearly fit that latter description!

Moving into this new apostolic paradigm, several second-generation denominational renewal leaders have gained the boldness to revisit the founders of their denominations. They have almost invariably discovered that their founders, many of them reluctantly, learned that it was impossible to transform their root denominations from old wineskins to new wineskins. Following in the footsteps of their founders, these second-generation leaders are now seeking ways of gracefully separating from past affiliations and pioneering new vehicles for charismatic and theological renewal. Some of them are ready to say, with Luther, "Here I stand; I can do no other!" They have the spiritual boldness to break the ungodly covenant with the corporate spirit of religion and to pay whatever price is necessary to do it.

IN SEVERAL DENOMINATIONAL COMMUNITIES WORLDWIDE, ENTIRE CONGREGATIONS HAVE DECIDED TO LEAVE THEIR DENOMINATIONS AND PLACE THEMSELVES UNDER THE LEADERSHIP OF A RENEWAL LEADER OF THEIR OWN DENOMINATIONAL BACKGROUND, A MODERN-DAY APOSTLE.

A WORLDWIDE MOVEMENT

Although I deal primarily with the American scene in this chapter, it is also worthy of mention that similar things are happening in other parts of the world. Here, for example, is a quote from a report from Fiji: "Large, Spirit-filled churches have really developed within the last few years. Many of these new churches have branched out from mainstream denominations such as the Methodists and the Assemblies of God movements. This shows that people are beginning to break out from the religious spirit and tradition that is still strong in many churches in Fiji."[8]

The new wineskin being shaped around the world is apostolic networks. In several denominational communities worldwide, renewal leaders are now founding associations of one kind or another to receive, not individuals, but entire renewed congregations that have decided corporately—both pastors and laypeople—to leave their denominations. In most cases, the congregations are placing themselves under the leadership of a renewal leader of their own denominational background. Whether the renewal leaders use the term or not, they are modern-day apostles who are among the vital leaders of the Second Apostolic Age.

A WIDESPREAD MOVEMENT

In Colorado Springs in 2003, over 20 American second-generation renewal leaders met with each other for the first time. For the most part, they had thought that they were oddballs for obeying God and withdrawing whole congregations from denominations and forming them into apostolic networks. They discovered, however, that they were part of a widespread movement of leaders who are hearing what the Spirit is saying to the churches. Represented around the table, for example, were Mennonite, United Methodist, Lutheran, Disciples of Christ, Episcopalian, Foursquare, Grace Brethren, Church of God (Cleveland), Evangelical Covenant and Assemblies of God.

One of the pioneers of this movement is Paul Anderson, whom Larry Christenson of Lutheran Renewal had chosen as his successor in 1995. Anderson soon came to the reluctant conclusion that the Lutheran Renewal was in serious decline within the Evangelical Lutheran Church in America. Together with some of the other younger leaders, he formed a Renewal Advisory Team, with the acronym RAT. He threw down the gauntlet by publishing a widely circulated article, "If the Ship Is Sinking."

By 1999, some of the renewal leaders had become thoroughly convinced that the Church could not be reformed from within. Paul Anderson secured the permission of the Lutheran Renewal board to establish two things: The first was a new network of congregations that wanted to move into a new wineskin of renewal. (Some congregations have chosen to withdraw their affiliation from ELCA while others have not taken that step.) The second was a new seminary for training clergy. Both have shown healthy growth. The network is called Alliance of Renewal Churches (ARC), and even non-Lutheran congregations are now seeking affiliation. The seminary has a strong student body, and Anderson's missionary vision is to plant similar seminaries in other countries around the world.

Another pioneer is Bishop Chuck Murphy, an Episcopal priest who, by the mid 1990s, had became completely disillusioned with the theological corruption of the leadership of his denomination. Efforts to bring about internal change were fruitless. The confirmation of an open-ly gay bishop in 2003 subsequently proved him right.

Murphy began the process by calling together 30 like-minded priests to form a group called First Promise. After two years of struggle, this group determined to form a new network of Episcopal congregations outside of the Episcopal Church, USA. Not surprisingly, American Episcopalian leaders would not consecrate a bishop for this upstart group, so the group went outside to the larger Anglican Communion. The archbishop of the Anglican Province of Rwanda and the archbishop of Southeast Asia, much to the discomfort of the Archbishop of Canterbury, decided to consecrate Chuck Murphy and John Rogers as missionary bishops and send them back to the United States as mis-sionaries to form and lead a new functional apostolic network called the Anglican Mission in America. In the first three years Bishop Murphy had received or planted 55 Episcopal congregations that affiliated with the network, and he reports that momentum has just begun to build. His goal is to plant biblically based Anglican (Episcopalian) churches throughout America and in other nations around the world.

A NEW APOSTOLIC DIRECTION

Similar stories are being told in denomination after denomination. A new generation of courageous leaders is now emerging. These are lead-ers who have decided to pay whatever price is necessary to break with the corporate spirit of religion that held them and their congregations in bondage. They are forming new wineskins to receive new wine from God. They are helping their people move from internal reform to apos-tolic renewal!

CHAPTER FOUR

FROM A CHURCH VISION TO A KINGDOM VISION

THE KINGDOM OF GOD IS NOT CONFINED TO THE FOUR WALLS OF THE LOCAL CHURCH.

This may be a simple statement to make, but it has enormous implications for the way we Christian leaders plan our focus for ministry. The old wineskin was church focused. The church was regarded as the center of gravity for the Christian life. One's commitment to Christ would be measured, at least to a significant degree, by whether one was a responsible member of a local church.

TWO TRADITIONAL PRESUPPOSITIONS

Many traditional church leaders, even today, would strongly affirm the following two presuppositions:

1. The work of ministry is done in the local church—in church-sponsored activities—or possibly in a parachurch organization.
2. The Body of Christ is the visible manifestation of the kingdom of God. Consequently, church leadership has been trained to carry out their responsibilities in the kingdom of God here on Earth primarily through the local church. Local church pastors will typically focus their efforts on the growth and health of their congregation, and denominational leaders will typically focus their efforts on the growth and health of the cluster of churches under their jurisdiction.

A change has begun. Growing numbers of leaders, most of whom began their ministry with these two traditional presuppositions, are beginning to enter a paradigm shift. They now regard what is done in conjunction with the local church as bona fide Kingdom activity but as only part of the whole picture. Most of them would trace the beginnings of this change back to the 1960s when the Holy Spirit began speaking to the churches about the social responsibility of the Body of Christ.

SOCIAL RESPONSIBILITY

Prior to the 1960s, evangelical leaders, by and large, did not regard social action as part of the Church's mission. Instead, they considered evangelism and church planting as the activities central to the mission. Their exclusion of social action came partly in reaction to the liberal wing of the Church, which, 50 years earlier, had all but replaced evangelism with social ministries.

The nature of this change in thinking can be clearly seen through the eyes of John R. W. Stott of England, widely regarded as one of the most influential evangelical theologians of this generation. At least until 1967, Stott's position was that "the commission of the church is not to reform society, but to preach the Gospel."[1] By 1975, however, Stott had experienced this paradigm shift, and he would write, "The word 'mission' . . . includes evangelism and social responsibility, since both are authentic expressions of love which longs to serve man in his need."[2]

As this understanding of what God expects His people to do has matured over the years, the concept of the kingdom of God has greatly expanded. No longer is it adequate to suppose that our ultimate task here on Earth is the growth of the Church. Church growth remains crucial, but the Kingdom goes beyond that. Our objective is encompassed in the prayer, "Your kingdom come. Your will be done on earth as it is in heaven" (Matt. 6:10).

A BROADENED CONCEPT OF MINISTRY

As we saw in the first traditional presupposition stated previously, to those of us who were trained in the old wineskin only what was done in the local churches was considered valid ministry, and what was done elsewhere was something else.

I illustrate this point with a quote from an advertisement by one of our most respected evangelical seminaries in one of our most respected Christian magazines. I will not mention names, because I do not wish to criticize either the magazine or the seminary. This is simply the standard way that most of us, including myself, have been programmed to think.

The seminary says in its ad, "Has God called you to the ministry? Though all Christians are called to serve the cause of Christ, God calls certain persons to serve the Church as pastors and other ministers. It is a high honor to be called of God into the ministry."

That is old wineskin language. In contrast, no one uses new wineskin language better than Ed Silvoso. Here are what Silvoso identifies as four lethal misbeliefs that minimize the impact of believers in the workplace:

1. There is a God-ordained division between clergy and laity.
2. The Church is called to operate primarily inside a building often referred to as the temple.
3. People involved in business cannot be as spiritual as those serving in traditional Church ministry.
4. The primary role of marketplace Christians is to make money to support the vision of those "in the ministry."[3]

An understanding of these broadens our understanding of ministry.

THE NEED TO RENEW THE MIND

As a part of the Second Apostolic Age, as I have said, the Holy Spirit is strongly speaking to the churches to initiate a paradigm shift from being church centered to being Kingdom centered. The central issue behind this shift is how we *think*. It is not so much our hearts as our minds that need to be changed if we desire to move into the new wineskin. The book of Romans says, "Do not be conformed to this world, but be transformed by the *renewing of your mind*, that you may prove what is that good and acceptable and perfect will of God" (12:2, emphasis added).

When a paradigm shift occurs, it is inevitable that some people will be pulled out of their comfort zones. Here is where the corporate spirit of religion can come into the picture. Since this may turn out to be one of the more radical paradigm shifts demanded in the Second Apostolic

Age, the spirit of religion will likely employ its tactic of belaw, the Hebrew word for wearing out people's minds, as I explained in chapter 1. Being transformed by the renewing of our minds is the last thing that the corporate spirit of religion desires. Rather, it attempts to manipulate our minds so that we strive to preserve the status quo. Resisting change is perceived as the will of God. The spell that this spirit casts forces us to do everything we can to prevent people from hearing what the Holy Spirit is saying to the churches.

I believe that there are six areas in our thinking that need to be fine-tuned in order to harmonize with the shift from being church centered to being Kingdom centered.

1. We Need to Understand the Kingdom

This is where we affirm that the kingdom of God is not confined to the four walls of the local church. Where is the kingdom of God? For one thing, it is not a kingdom of this world. It cannot join the United Nations. It has no territorial boundaries. It does not issue passports. Rather, the kingdom of God is present wherever individual men and women have agreed that Jesus Christ is their Lord. All who regard God as their King are citizens of the kingdom of God. Jesus said to His followers, "The kingdom of God is within you" (Luke 17:21).

God's desire for the human race is that every man, woman and child receive His blessings. He wants people to be happy and prosperous. He wants them to be healthy and at peace. His designated agents to bring this about are those of us who acknowledge Jesus as Lord. We are the ones who pray, "Your kingdom come. Your will be done on earth as it is in heaven." And God will answer that prayer to a large extent by working through His people, individuals like you and me.

The goal of our service to God in this life, then, must be nothing less than the transformation of society. I will mention this from time to time in this chapter, but transforming society is so important for the Second Apostolic Age that I will go into much more detail in a chapter devoted to the subject.

2. We Need to Understand That There Is a Church in the Workplace

I feel that the major step in moving from a church vision to a Kingdom vision will be to expand our traditional concept of the Church.

The biblical word translated "Church" is *ekklesia*. Its root meaning is the people of God. Sometimes "ekklesia" is used in the New Testament to signify the people of God meeting together. And then sometimes it is used to signify believers in a general sense wherever they might be—gathered or scattered.

WHERE IS THE KINGDOM OF GOD? IT IS PRESENT WHEREVER INDIVIDUAL MEN AND WOMEN HAVE AGREED THAT JESUS CHRIST IS THEIR LORD.

Where, then, do you find the true ekklesia? One day a week you find it gathered together in local congregations representing many different denominations. But six days a week, the people of God are scattered out in the workplace. Denominational lines do not make as much difference six days a week as they do when God's people meet together. We need to recognize that the people of God are the people of God all seven days of the week.

Whenever we find ourselves entering into a paradigm shift, terminology becomes very important. I remember talking about this to Leo Lawson of Morningstar International; his terminology helped renew my mind. Using the sociological parallel of the nuclear family and the extended family, Leo suggested that we call the Church that meets together in local congregations the nuclear Church and the Church scattered throughout the workplace the extended Church. This is extremely useful terminology because, being new, it does not bring with it a lot of the baggage we have accumulated in our minds.

If we can learn to see the Church from this perspective, we have begun to move toward a Kingdom perspective. Many of us, quite properly, have our membership in a local church. But we must keep in mind that our church membership is not our Kingdom membership. Our Kingdom membership is in the Church that exists all seven days of the week wherever the people of God might be found.

Let me take a moment to stress how important the renewing of the mind is to the definition of "Church." David Oliver in *Church That Works* warns us that we are in a battle over these issues. In this book is a chapter called "Whoever Gets the Name 'Church' Wins."[4] Oliver believes that those of us who desire to broaden the traditional definition of "Church" are up against a mind-set that is a spiritual stronghold. He doesn't mention the spirit of religion, but I am sure that it is what he is describing.

Oliver points out that when Jesus said that He would build His Church, He set it in the context of giving the keys of the kingdom of heaven to Peter, on whom the Church would be founded (see Matt. 16:18-19). Oliver goes on to say,

> The church is set in the context of the Kingdom—the rule of God through all creation—earth and heaven. . . . [The kingdom] is the overarching link between the two realms, and the church is the agent by which those keys turn to open or shut, to release or bind.[5]

If our broadened definition of "Church," which includes both the nuclear Church and the extended Church, is true—and I firmly believe it is—it has four huge implications:

1. Each of the Churches, the nuclear Church and the extended Church, has a distinct culture. Peter Tsukahira, the pastor of a Messianic congregation in Israel, says, "Culture contains values and expectations that lie beneath our conscious thoughts. There is a church culture and there is a business culture. Although the two coexist in the believing community, it is as

if they have different values and goals, speak different languages, and have entirely different customs."[6]

2. The cultural gap is enormous. When I began to study ministry in the workplace, I knew there were different cultures, but I had no idea how huge the gap was until I read the sociological study *Church on Sunday, Work on Monday* by Laura Nash and Scotty McLennan (Jossey-Bass).

3. Each culture has its own rule book—this is simply "Anthropology 101."

4. Most extended Church leaders understand both rule books, while most nuclear Church leaders understand only one rule book.

When these four thoughts become more widely known, it will not be difficult to predict how the spirit of religion will work to try to block the paradigm shift from church thinking to Kingdom thinking.

3. We Need to Understand that Christian Ministry Is Not Confined to the Nuclear Church

Let me repeat one of the traditional presuppositions with which I began this chapter: The work of ministry is done in the local church—in church-sponsored activities—or possibly in parachurch organizations. This effectively restricts Christian ministry to the one percent of believers who are ordained ministers. Or if we include so-called laypeople who have official ministries in churches, a generous estimate might be that 20 percent do what has been traditionally thought of as "the ministry."

But Ephesians 4:12 indicates that the ones who are supposed to do the work of the ministry are the saints—100 percent of believers. The new paradigm concludes that we don't do the work of the ministry just one day a week when we are in church but that we do it seven days a week. What we do in the workplace Monday through Saturday is ministry. Believers who are bus drivers, nurses, lawyers, schoolteachers, carpenters, corporate CEOs and the like are all engaged in ministry as they go about work.

Is this biblical? Yes. The Greek word translated "ministry" is *diakonia*. But this word is also translated "service" in the New Testament. So whenever you are serving others in the name of the Lord by waiting on customers in a restaurant or filling teeth or fixing tires, you are ministering to others. Ministry takes place in the extended Church just as much as it does in the nuclear Church.

When does a "job" become a ministry? It becomes a ministry when God leads you into the area and you take the voice of God, the anointing of God and biblical principles with you as you work and minister.

Another important implication of this concept relates to the awkward term "parachurch ministries." The word "parachurch" implies that the organization is not quite good enough to be called a church; the comparison is similar to that of an inaccurate comparison between a paralegal and a lawyer. Some nuclear Church leaders have even gone on record as saying that parachurch ministries are God's Plan B. His Plan A, in their view, would be that nuclear churches should be carrying out the functions of parachurch ministries, but because nuclear churches have defaulted, parachurch organizations are acceptable as a stopgap measure.

Until now, it has not seemed appropriate for parachurch organizations to identify with the workplace for fear that they might be considered worldly or unspiritual or not part of the Church at all, even though they function just like companies in the workplace. Some are huge nonprofit companies such as Campus Crusade, Focus on the Family and the Billy Graham Evangelistic Association. Some, like Strang Communications and John Maxwell's Injoy, have not felt this inhibition about seeming worldly, and they are incorporated as for-profit companies. Now that we understand that the extended Church operates in the workplace, parachurch organizations can see themselves in a legitimate extended Church ministry that offers services and sells goods to the nuclear Church. No longer is one "the Church" and the other something else.[7]

4. We Need to Understand That the Church Has a God-Designed Government

This is a book on the Second Apostolic Age. One of the major premises that has brought me to this subject is that the foundation of the Church is apostles and prophets, as the Bible says in Ephesians 2:20, and that these apostles and prophets exist today. They are part of God-designed church government.

MANY OF GOD'S PEOPLE IN THE WORKPLACE HAVE DONE THEIR BEST TO BE SALT AND LIGHT IN THEIR WORKPLACE FOR 10 OR 20 YEARS AND NOTHING HAS CHANGED. WHY?

Logically, God's design for church government would apply to the whole Church. This means that, just as there are apostles and prophets in the nuclear Church, we would also expect to find apostles and prophets in the extended Church.

God's people in the workplace know that they are "salt" and "light" (Matt. 5:13-16). They have been taught this since day one in the nuclear Church. However, many of them have done their best to be salt and light in their workplace for 10 or 20 years and nothing has changed. Why? The answer might lie in the fact that the spiritual government of the extended Church has not yet come into place. Recognized apostles are not yet setting things in order in the workplace.

I believe that things will change rapidly once we begin to identify and support the ministry of apostles in the workplace. Admittedly, most of the work done to date on apostles and apostolic ministry has focused on the nuclear Church. Now we must move from the local church to the Kingdom and figure out how apostles are supposed to function in the extended Church. Bill Hamon has made a pioneering contribution to this process in his book *The Day of the Saints* (Destiny Image), in which he dedicates 82 pages to the work of apostles, prophets, evangelists, pastors and teachers in the workplace. I recommend this book for those seeking further information on these subjects.

5. We Need to Understand the Full Scope of the Word "Workplace"
Once again I will reiterate that terminology helps define the pathway in a paradigm shift. A considerable body of literature has been developing around what some call the faith and work movement. These authors are attempting to inform the Body of Christ that believers do ministry outside of the local church as well as inside it. In this literature, you will see that the terms "marketplace" and "workplace" are used interchangeably. However, more recently a consensus has begun to develop among leaders in the field that "workplace" may be the more useful term, because, by itself, it is more inclusive. In the minds of many, "marketplace" connotes the buying and selling of goods. "Workplace" more naturally includes all types of work, such as parenting, teaching, dentistry, bus driving, governing and auto repair.

Apostles, whether in the nuclear Church or the extended Church, exercise authority only in God-assigned spheres. Paul says, "We, however, will not boast [of our authority] beyond measure, but within the limits of the sphere which God appointed us—a sphere which especially includes you" (2 Cor. 10:13).

In the workplace, what would the spheres look like? It seems logical that they would be areas such as finance, technology, medicine, industry, education, motherhood, homemaking, transportation, agriculture, military, government, law, communications, business, athletics and so on.

We could expect that God would raise up apostles for the government of the Church in each one of these spheres. When you think of it, each sphere has a slightly different rule book. For example, an apostle in one sphere, such as athletics, might not know the rule book of another, such as agriculture.

6. We Need to Be Fully Aware of the Two Strategic Gates for the Advance of the Kingdom of God That Will Be Opened Through the Ministry of Apostles in the Workplace

I deal with this sixth point only in passing because I examine it in detail in chapter 6. There I explain why workplace apostles are crucial if these two gates for advancing the kingdom of God are to be opened:

- **The gate of social transformation.** We now have a long enough track record of attempting to transform society without seeing any of the cities that we have targeted actually being transformed. Something is probably missing.
- **The gate of the transference of wealth.** Credible prophecies have declared that God is poised to release unprecedented amounts of wealth for the expansion of His kingdom. Is there something that He is waiting for before He allows this to happen?

Two Cultures, Two Rule Books

Let's go back to perhaps the most crucial point in this chapter, namely the fact that the nuclear Church and the extended Church operate out of two separate cultural rule books. For the next several years a good deal of debate, dialogue, disagreement and conflict will, more than likely, surface among church leaders over this very issue.

When we discuss cultures, we must keep in mind that, anthropologically speaking, culture is a value-neutral concept. This is not to ignore the fact that every known human culture has been corrupted by the Fall and contaminated by sinful elements. Despite this fact, there are many behavior patterns in a given culture that are not to be regarded as either better or worse than behavior patterns in a different culture. Take, for example, the American and the Japanese cultures. In America we eat with forks; in Japan they eat with chopsticks. We drive on the right; they drive on the left. We leave our shoes on when we go into a house; they take them off. We buy with dollars; they buy with yen. Which one is right? American culture is right for Americans; Japanese culture is right for Japanese. Neither one should be seen as wrong.

Conflict only surfaces when individuals from two cultures begin to interact with each other. For example, the Japanese culture is a gift-giving culture, while the American culture is not. The Japanese rule book says that it is appropriate to give a gift to a person with whom you hope to complete a business deal. The American culture attaches pejorative labels, such as "kickbacks" or "bribes," to those gifts. At points like this, Americans are inclined to think that the Japanese are wrong and that they should really be more like us.

Although it is not a pleasant thought, the potential for conflict between nuclear Church leaders and extended Church leaders over issues related to Church culture is very high. As I have said, most extended Church leaders understand both rule books because they follow one six days a week and the other one day a week. However, some nuclear Church leaders will likely deny that there are two rule books for the Church, or if they do recognize the two rule books, they might well dispute the idea that the rules in each book are value-neutral.

THE CORPORATE SPIRIT OF RELIGION

This seems to be shaping up as an easy field of operation for the corporate spirit of religion. The paradigm of *Kingdom* thinking, rather than *church* thinking, is part of the new wineskin. The spirit of religion will do anything it can to prevent those who are comfortable in the old wineskin from renewing their minds and entering the new wineskin.

I like the way James Thwaites, author of *Renegotiating the Church Contract*, describes how this happens. He explains his belief that many church leaders are now beginning to sincerely desire to support their workplace members in a more meaningful way than they have previously supported them. But then he comments,

When these leaders attempt to release the saints into their life and work by changing the culture of church they come under pressure to keep the church the way it has been. When they set out to equip the saints to salt, light and leaven their world they find themselves limited by the constraints of a bounded church culture.[8]

Although Thwaites doesn't make the overt connection, this is exactly how the corporate spirit of religion operates.

A NEW APOSTOLIC DIRECTION

We are only now in the beginning stages of moving from a church vision to a Kingdom vision. It will take a while, but I believe that the Second Apostolic Age will be characterized by a much more powerful Church and a much more rapidly advancing Kingdom than any of us has ever seen. One of its most exciting features will be the full activation of the Church in the workplace.

CHAPTER FIVE

FROM HERITAGE-BASED CHURCH ALIGNMENT TO TERRITORIAL CHURCH ALIGNMENT

ONE THING THAT HAS SURPRISED ME AS I HAVE INTER-
ACTED WITH AMERICAN CHURCH LEADERS OVER THE
YEARS IS THE LIMITED NUMBER OF CONTACTS THAT MANY
OF THEM HAVE WITH PEERS OUTSIDE OF THEIR OWN
DENOMINATION.

DENOMINATIONAL DIFFERENCES

For a number of years, I led the Fuller Institute for Evangelism and
Church Growth and worked as a consultant with churches across a wide
denominational spectrum. Since I was not brought up in a Christian
home, ecclesiastical tradition had never been part of my personal identity. My wife, Doris, and I have always maintained membership in a local
church, but in no case did we choose the church because of the denomination to which it happened to be affiliated. As we have moved from
place to place, we have been, for example, Methodist, Baptist, Bible
Church, Quaker and Congregationalist.

I say this to explain, at least in part, why I found it relatively easy to
move from denomination to denomination as a consultant. For 33
years, I have been a faculty member of Fuller Theological Seminary, a
school that serves multiple denominations. My day-to-day contacts were
with leaders from vastly differing church heritages, and we all seemed to
get along well with each other as long as we stayed in the interdenomi-
national environment. In my Doctor of Ministry classes, which were
made up of pastors and other leaders from approximately 50 denominations, I developed the supposition that building relationships across
denominational lines, as we were doing at Fuller, was the norm. How
wrong I was! Once I began moving into the leadership circles of specific
denominations, I found quite a difference.

Take, for example, heroes. Most denominations have compiled a list
of acceptable heroes. I found that with the Salvation Army it helps to
refer to General Booth. With Assemblies of God, mention Stanley
Horton. Foursquare members like to hear the name of Jack Hayford.
Talk about Luther with Lutherans, Wesley with Methodists and Calvin

with Presbyterians and you are on safe ground. However, if you refer to an authority not on the list of denominational heroes, your comments will likely be regarded as irrelevant. Why? Simply because most denominational people never will have heard of the heroes honored in other denominations.

HERITAGE-BASED DENOMINATIONS

It is easy to suppose that the major differences between denominations lie in doctrines or church practices. For example, Episcopalians baptize infants while Baptists dedicate infants. Nazarenes look for a "second blessing" of sanctification while Assemblies of God look for a "second blessing" in Spirit baptism with tongues. Congregationalists believe that each local church should be autonomous while Methodists believe they should be connected.

However, few sociologists of religion would agree that the primary differences are doctrinal. Over 70 years ago, pioneer sociologist H. Richard Niebuhr wrote in his book, *The Social Sources of Denominationalism*, "Denominations . . . are sociological groups whose principle of differentiation is to be sought in their conformity to the order of social classes and castes."[1] Keeping in mind that denominations were birthed through the European settlement of America, consider what historian Russell Richey has to say: "Denominations came to bear functions . . . that in European society were carried out by kin-groups, the village, local religious and civil authorities, and the culture."[2]

The ethnicity of the denomination has been a major factor throughout America's history. Despite strenuous efforts at integrating denominations over the past 40 years, the truly multiethnic church is still a relatively rare phenomenon. I recall hearing a while ago a report from researcher and author Mike Regele; he had found that of all commonalities of Presbyterian congregations in Southern California, Scottish ancestry ranked as number one. Ethnicity, rather than theology, is the basis of differentiation between these Presbyterians and, for example, Church of God in Christ, one of America's larger African-American denominations. Even in the strongly Lutheran North Central states, many clusters of Lutheran congregations are held together by their German ethnicity, while other Lutheran congregations are held together by their Scandinavian ancestry. Even more, certain Norwegian Lutheran leaders rarely connect with neighboring Swedish Lutheran leaders.

Why do I point this out? It is to show us why, in the old wineskin, denominational leaders have maintained most of their religious, professional, social, familial and recreational lives within the boundaries of their own denominations. This may not have been as true of the laity, especially over the past 20 or 30 years, as it has been of the clergy, if I may for a moment revert to that passé clergy-laity terminology. But for the most part, denominational pastors went to the same schools, attend the same meetings, educate their children in the same way, plan social functions with each other, read the same literature, vote for the same political party and marry spouses from the same denominational heritage.

Because of the social cohesion within a denominational heritage, most pastors in a city have associated primarily, and sometimes exclusively, with pastors from their same denomination. Typically in a given city, Baptist pastors have known very few Lutheran pastors, who have known very few Assemblies of God pastors, who have known very few Nazarene pastors, who have known very few Presbyterian pastors, and so on.

Most church members belong to the denomination of their parents. It is part of their heritage. In the old wineskin, church members who moved to a new city would look for a church of their denomination for church membership. And many members, Sunday after Sunday, would drive past 10 or 20 other churches in order to attend the one of their own denomination.

THE OLD-WINESKIN MENTALITY

I believe that part of the overall strategy of the corporate spirit of religion is to preserve this heritage-based church alignment. It reminds me of the Pharisees who once asked Jesus, "Why do Your disciples not walk according to the tradition of the elders?" (Mark 7:5). Jesus, who was forming a new wineskin, responded, "All too well you reject the commandment of God, that you may keep your tradition" (Mark 7:9). I repeat what I have said more than once, namely that I am not contending that denominations are bad. For a time they were God's new wineskins. Large numbers of people will choose to remain in the old wineskins, and for many it is a good choice. God loves them and He will bless them, but the trade-off is that they won't receive new wine. I am simply attempting to clarify the options for those who might be willing to consider making the changes necessary to receive God's new wine.

Church historian Elwyn Smith puts his finger on the activity of the spirit of religion (my term, not Smith's) when he affirms that one of the constitutive elements of American denominationalism is "a conservative, sometimes legalistic, determination to maintain a distinctive identity in the face of change."[3] To show how this works out in real life, the following quote is from an official directive from a certain denominational headquarters to the pastors of its churches across America: "Choose your pulpit guests wisely. Going outside the list of recognized credential holders of our fellowship can bring undesired teachings and example." I recognize that a role of pastors is to protect the people in their care, but I disagree with a denomination that becomes ingrown and refuses to allow its pastors to interact with the wider Body of Christ.

Such legalistic church alignment is clearly not a thing of the past. The previously quoted directive was sent out as late as the year 2000. Change is still a serious threat to many.

To summarize the old-wineskin mentality: "Let's not change. Let's stick to our heritage!"

TERRITORIAL APOSTOLIC CHURCHES

Old-wineskin leaders may not want to change, but the new wineskin is here. This may have to do with the postmodern generation and their notable aversion to brand loyalty. Now when church people move to a new city, most of them are not as interested in finding a church of their own denomination as their parents might have been. In fact, many parents are less interested than they used to be as well. This is one of the reasons why such a large percentage of megachurch growth in America is due to transfer growth, not conversion growth.

IT IS NOW AS LIKELY THAT LOCAL CHURCH PASTORS WILL ESTABLISH THEIR PRIMARY PROFESSIONAL RELATIONSHIPS WITH OTHER PASTORS OF THEIR CITY AS THEY WILL WITH DENOMINATIONAL COLLEAGUES OUTSIDE OF THE CITY.

Although the trend can be traced back to the early 1990s, territory is now becoming more important than heritage for many leaders. Joseph Mattera, an apostle from New York City, observes that in these times of the Second Apostolic Age, "Bible-believing pastors and ministers voluntarily come together regionally to advance the kingdom of God, irrespective of their denominational affiliation and sectarian identities."[4] It is now as likely that local church pastors will establish their primary professional relationships with other pastors of their city as they will with denominational colleagues outside of the city. In fact, some pastors have much less interest in attending regional and national denominational meetings than they used to. The city meetings have higher priority for them.

This trend has a very interesting corollary. Here is how Joseph Mattera puts it: "Ministerial leaders emerge who have an 'apostolic anointing' to galvanize the body of Christ in their region, and give direction to the city church government."[5] My term for these individuals is "territorial apostles." They are apostles, one of whose God-assigned spheres is a geographical territory—more than likely a city but possibly a region or even a nation. Some of these territorial apostles will be nuclear

Church apostles, but others—perhaps the majority—will be extended Church (or workplace) apostles.

As soon as we understand this, a high-potential area for the activity of the corporate spirit of religion becomes clear. Some regional denominational executives could begin to discover that certain pastors under their jurisdiction are developing a divided loyalty. Mattera goes on to say,

> This scares some denominational leaders who exercise leadership over certain ministers and churches only because of political placement, organizational loyalty, seniority, and/or administrative ability. . . . Opposition against the apostolic will most likely be fueled more because certain religious leaders believe it will undermine the influence they have in a region—not because of theological disagreement.[6]

A CASE STUDY: GUILDFORD, ENGLAND

To make these principles as practical as possible, let's look at a real-life situation in Guildford, England, where much of what we have been saying is actually taking place.

One of the workplace apostles who has taken membership in the International Coalition of Apostles (ICA), of which I serve as a leader, is Julian Watts. He is in the process of developing a large international company, Markets Unlocked. Backed by sophisticated state-of-the art electronics, Markets Unlocked is designed to facilitate mutually beneficial business opportunities across international boundaries. Watts's focus is connecting Israeli businesses with entrepreneurs in each of America's 50 states. The home base of his company is Guildford, England.

Guildford is located at the heart of Surrey's stockbroker belt and is a very affluent community. At the same time, it has gained an unenviable reputation for extravagant me-first materialism, and worse yet, it carries the stigma of being rated by some as the divorce capital of Europe.

Territorial Alignment

During the decade of the 1990s, about a dozen Guildford pastors of various denominations began to pray together and to build strong, committed personal relationships with each other. They were an example of beginning to move from what I am calling heritage-based church alignment to territorial alignment. In 2002, they invited a healing evangelist from New Zealand to hold a week of citywide healing meetings in Guildford. The meetings were so successful that they asked him to stay for two more weeks. He had a previous obligation for the following week, but he agreed to return for the two weeks after that.

Now the pastors had a problem. How do they adequately prepare, in just one week, for this large citywide event? They had no clue, but fortunately God did. God clearly spoke to Julian Watts to put his international business dealings to one side for two weeks and to give himself entirely to the city. Julian, a high-energy, successful entrepreneur, at first thought that God must be kidding. But after a rather sharp dialogue with God, he found that God was dead serious, so Julian wisely decided to obey. One thing that helped a bit was that the healing evangelist also happened to be—or perhaps divinely arranged—the New Zealand national representative for Markets Unlocked.

The City of the Bride

None of the sponsoring pastors had either training or experience as a project manager. Julian had both, and he had seen success in the workplace. The pastors welcomed his offer for help, so Watts took over. God had also revealed to him that He had designated Guildford as the City of the Bride, and that Markets Unlocked would be part of the Bride. With this in mind, Julian did what was necessary in the city to prepare the way for the healing meetings that ended up surpassing the expectations of the conveners and making a tremendous impact on the city.

Through this process, as would be expected, Julian bonded with the pastors. What happened, in my analysis, could be a prototype for things to come worldwide. The Guildford leaders might use different language to describe what had happened, but here is the way I see it: A group of nuclear Church leaders heard from God concerning the transformation of their city. They put denominational differences to one side and coalesced territorially—the theme of this chapter. As they prayed together, they heard what the Spirit was saying to the churches of their city. But they also recognized, through a divinely ordered set of circumstances, that their pastoral giftings could take them only so far. They knew that they needed something else.

What they needed was an apostle. They might not have used that word, nor would they have been aware that their neighbor Julian Watts had already been recognized as an apostle by the International Coalition of Apostles. Watts was regarded by ICA, not as a *nuclear Church* apostle, but rather as an *extended Church* (or workplace) apostle. This means that he would have a set of apostolic skills, such as acting as a project manager for the healing event, that the nuclear Church leaders—even what nuclear Church apostles there might have been among them—would in all probability not possess.

Territorial Authority

Until that point, Julian had been ministering with apostolic authority in the international business world, but he did not have territorial authority in Guildford. In fact, he had never even desired it until he heard directly from God that Guildford was to be the City of the Bride and that he was to have a role in seeing that God's will was accomplished there. That is where apostolic protocol entered the picture. Julian would have made a serious mistake if he had gone out from there and proclaimed himself a territorial apostle. However, he didn't take that course because, by nature, he is a servant leader. His only action at the time was to serve the group of 12 pastors and enable them to fulfill the vision that God had given them.

But by the time the immediate task of the evangelistic event was done, the pastors had accepted Julian as one of them. He became the only noncongregationally-based member of the group. The nuclear

Church leaders had expanded their inner circle by adding an extended Church leader. Or to look at it from another perspective, a group of pastors had invited an apostle to join them.

Once Julian began meeting with the pastors, he began casting the vision of Guildford as the City of the Bride. He suggested that the group agree to test this idea with their church leaders. Since the pastors had not been accustomed to dealing with what some of us call the redemptive gifts of cities, the process of accepting Julian's suggestion took them three months of serious discussion. But once they were ready, they asked Julian to speak to a citywide cross-denominational meeting. Julian tried to decline the offer, but the pastors insisted and he finally agreed.

An Apostolic Declaration

As he was preparing for the meeting, Watts felt that the Lord was asking him to make an apostolic declaration. An apostolic declaration is a form of intercession in which apostles first receive a clear direction from God. Then, confident that they are seeing what the Father is doing (see John 5:19), they do not petition God, but rather they declare His will into being. Watts felt that, at the cross-denominational meeting in Guildford, he should proclaim Isaiah 61:10—62:4 for Guildford.

Keeping in mind that Guildford's disgrace has been having one of the highest divorce rates in Europe but that Guildford's redemptive gift was to be the City of the Bride, look at how this Scripture fits like a glove:

> I will greatly rejoice in the LORD, my soul shall be joyful in my God; for He has clothed me with the garments of salvation, He has covered me with the robe of righteousness. As a bridegroom decks himself with ornaments, and *as a bride adorns herself with her jewels*. For [Guildford's] sake I will not hold My peace, and for [Guildford's] sake I will not rest, until her righteousness goes forth as brightness, and her salvation as a lamp that burns. The [nations] shall see your righteousness, and all kings your glory. You shall be called by a new name ["City of the Bride"], which

the mouth of the LORD will name. You shall no longer be termed Forsaken, nor shall your land any more be termed Desolate; but you shall be called Hephzibah, and your land Beulah [which means in Hebrew "married"]; for the LORD delights in you, and *your land shall be married* (61:10; 62:1-2,4, emphasis added).

This apostolic declaration that a city once known for divorce would end up happily married made a notable spiritual impact on the church leaders of Guildford. The pastors began inviting Julian Watts to speak at their churches' Sunday services. Julian would agree to speak, but only under the condition that afterwards he would pray for the people and ask God to impart the intimacy of a bride to the congregation. When he gave the altar call, it would not be unusual for the whole congregation to come forward. At times, the prayer ministry would last for two hours. Julian reports that during ministry time he would especially have to deal with delivering individuals from a spirit of Freemasonry and a spirit of pornography. The Bride was being cleansed.

THE STORY OF JULIAN WATTS PROVIDES A REAL-LIFE MODEL OF HOW THE ANOINTING OF AN APOSTLE CAN HELP A WHOLE COMMUNITY MOVE INTO ITS GOD-ORDAINED DESTINY.

The 12 pastors soon began to share Julian's message about the City of the Bride with some of the less active pastors of the city, and as a result, their group doubled in size. They scheduled a week-long, citywide prayer meeting, and they set aside the following Valentine's Day for the first public celebration of God's new destiny for Guildford.

A NEW APOSTOLIC DIRECTION

It is, of course, too early to know to what degree Guildford will see social transformation in the days to come. Nevertheless, the beginning of the process at least provides us a real-life model of how the anointing of an apostle—in this case a workplace apostle who then became a territorial apostle—can help a whole community move into its God-ordained destiny.

CHAPTER SIX

FROM THE EXPANSION OF THE CHURCH TO THE TRANSFORMATION OF SOCIETY

I CLEARLY REMEMBER MY WAKE-UP CALL. IT CAME IN A REVIEW BY MY FRIEND RAY BAKKE OF MY BOOK *CHURCH GROWTH AND THE WHOLE GOSPEL* (HARPER AND ROW). IN THE REVIEW, WHICH WAS GENERALLY FAVORABLE, RAY EXPRESSED HIS SURPRISE THAT IN A BOOK DEALING WITH THE SOCIAL RESPONSIBILITY OF THE CHURCH, I HAD NOT ONCE MENTIONED THE KINGDOM OF GOD.

When I read that, I immediately thought that Ray, a fellow seminary professor, must be wrong. So I went back over my book page by page. He turned out to be right! I had written an entire book on how the Church relates to society without including a single thought about how the Church relates to the kingdom of God.

I actually wrote Bakke a letter, thanking him for doing me a favor and calling me on the carpet. That was back in 1981. Since then, in just about every book I've written, I have intentionally related my message to the vital theme of the kingdom of God.

A KINGDOM FOCUS

This book is no exception. Let me pause and be specific at this point so that readers do not miss this important thought. For a starter, the whole institution of the Second Apostolic Age must be seen overall as a sovereign action of God for the expansion of His kingdom. In this book, chapters 4 through 7 give the kingdom of God a higher profile than other chapters do. Chapter 4 is entitled "From a Church Vision to a Kingdom Vision." It explains that the kingdom of God includes the extended (or workplace) Church, as well as the more traditional nuclear Church, which meets together weekly in a local church. Chapter 5 showed that some Christian leaders are beginning to look beyond their traditional denominational heritage to focus on their assigned geographical territory. This chapter, chapter 6, deals with societal transformation, and chapter 7 shows how spiritual warfare relates to the advance of the kingdom of God.

I will admit that, at the time of Bakke's wake-up call, I had been entirely focused on the Church—and with a passion. My academic role at Fuller Seminary was Professor of *Church* Growth. Yes, I had enough theological savvy to know better than to identify the nuclear Church with the kingdom of God. Many organizations that go by the name "Church" are as far from the kingdom of God today as the Pharisees were in Jesus' day. Also, the kingdom of God is much broader than the nuclear Church because it penetrates society as a whole. While I knew this, my passion for the nuclear Church had not allowed me much room for concentrating on the Kingdom and its role in society. I definitely was suffering from blind spots when I wrote *Church Growth and the Whole Gospel.*

THE KINGDOM OF GOD INCLUDES THE EXTENDED (OR WORKPLACE) CHURCH, AS WELL AS THE MORE TRADITIONAL NUCLEAR CHURCH, WHICH MEETS TOGETHER WEEKLY IN A LOCAL CHURCH.

THE IMPORTANCE OF CHURCH GROWTH

Nothing in these chapters should be taken to imply that I am trivializing the growth of the Church in any way. On the contrary, to trivialize Church growth would be to ignore one of Jesus' prime reasons for coming to Earth. He said to His disciples, "I will build My church" (Matt. 16:18). He commanded them to "preach the gospel to every creature" (Mark 16:15). And His Great Commission was to "make disciples of all the nations, baptizing them in the name of the Father and of the Son and of the Holy Spirit" (Matt. 28:19). When unbelievers become disciples of Jesus, they automatically become members of His Church. As I explained in chapter 4, the biblical word for "Church," ekklesia, simply means the people of God.

Most of God's people worldwide have made their commitment to Christ tangible through being baptized and through joining a local church.

When Jesus said, "I will build My church," He immediately connected it with the kingdom of God. He then went on to say, "The gates of Hades shall not prevail against it [because I am giving] you the keys of the kingdom of heaven" (Matt. 16:18-19). Whenever He sent His disciples out, He instructed them to "preach the kingdom of God" (Luke 9:2). After His resurrection, during His last 40 days here on Earth, Jesus taught His apostles about the kingdom of God (see Acts 1:3). And He concluded their final training session by telling them that, after He left, the Holy Spirit would come and give them power to be witnesses for Him (see Acts 1:8), presumably witnesses of the kingdom of God, which Jesus brought to Earth.

SIGNS OF THE KINGDOM

Of the many physical manifestations, or signs, that the kingdom of God is actually here on Earth, the local church is number one. This is not just any church. There are churches in which people worship idols. There are churches that do not believe the Bible. There are churches that, as Paul might say, "preach [another] gospel" (Gal. 1:8). There are churches that openly flaunt biblical morality. There are churches that wink at occult practices such as New Age. These churches, and others like them, are clearly not valid signs of God's kingdom.

But churches characterized by vibrant, life-giving Christianity, churches in which people love and sincerely worship God, churches that demonstrate compassion for the poor and needy, churches that facilitate the communication of the gospel to all nations, churches that see personal lives and families transformed by the power of the Holy Spirit, churches that maintain high standards of biblical morality—these churches indisputably are signs of the kingdom of God.

But they are not the only signs. One of the mistakes that I had been making in my enthusiasm for the nuclear Church was thinking that once a local church had been established and was growing and unbelievers were getting converted, we had done our job, so to speak. The Second Apostolic Age is inexorably changing this shortsighted mind-set. Preaching and living the kingdom of God certainly includes Church growth, but it goes considerably beyond that to the extension of the Kingdom in all of its multiple manifestations, which includes righteousness, economic sufficiency, freedom, morality, health and peaceful living.

HOW SHOULD EXPECTING A LITERAL ANSWER TO THE PRAYER "YOUR KINGDOM COME. YOUR WILL BE DONE ON EARTH AS IT IS IN HEAVEN" AFFECT OUR LIVES AND MINISTRIES?

THE KINGDOM ON EARTH

It is strange that it took some of us so long to see this. We all were in the habit of praying the prayer that Jesus taught us: "Your kingdom come. Your will be done on earth as it is in heaven" (Matt. 6:10). But only recently have many of us begun to understand how expecting a literal answer to this prayer should affect our lives and ministries.

There were several key leaders, especially through the 1990s, whom God used to help change our thinking. One of the first was John Dawson with his best-seller, *Taking Our Cities for God* (Creation House). The idea of *taking a city* was quite a departure from planting and multiplying churches in the city, although it didn't exclude that. Then came George Otis, Jr., who wrote a series of books on spiritual mapping, culminating in *Informed Intercession* (Regal Books). He then produced the legendary *Transformations* video, which documents the work of God around the world with such authenticity that thousands of people acquired a Kingdom mentality. Finally, Ed Silvoso nailed it down for us with *That*

None Should Perish (Regal Books) and *Prayer Evangelism* (Regal Books).

As we who were giving direction to the global prayer movement followed these leaders and attempted to make practical applications of their insights, we began to use terms such as "city reaching," "city taking," "city transformation" and then "regional transformation." Occasionally it escalated to "transformation of a nation," and one of my friends even began praying for "continental transformation." There is a growing consensus now that the most appropriate phraseology to include all of the above might be "social transformation." I like the way that Alistair Petrie puts it in his outstanding book that summarizes much of what we have been learning, *Transformed! Peoples, Cities, Nations*: "Authentic revival should lead to transformation, which is a continual process of people and society being changed into an ever-deepening relationship with God."[1]

PROGRESS TOWARD SOCIAL TRANSFORMATION

Let's take a look at the progress we have made toward social transformation and also at our goal for the future.

A Clear Direction

As I have said, we now have a consensus as to the direction that we are headed. Those participating in the new wineskin of the Second Apostolic Age continue aggressive evangelism and church planting, but they also pray for and work toward the transformation of society. We know what our goal is: that God's kingdom will come and His will shall be done on Earth as it is in heaven. We have the desire to see it happen, not someday, but in our own generation.

A New Set of Tools

Not only can we visualize the goal, but we also have many tools for accomplishing the task—tools that we did not even know about only a few years ago. We now know, for example, how to do spiritual mapping, identificational repentance, apostolic and prophetic intercession, prayer-walking, strategic-level spiritual warfare and the like. We have a National Prayer Committee, a National Day of Prayer coordinated by 8,000 people across the nation and a nationally broadcast Concert of Prayer, all of which focus on social transformation. We have attained an unprecedented degree of unity among Christian leaders of many of our cities and regions through Pastors' Prayer Summits and ministerial fellowships.

We in the United States have a functional Strategic Prayer Network (USSPN), which is led by my colleague Chuck Pierce. With 50 state coordinators, several regional coordinators and thousands of registered intercessors in each state, our ability to mobilize targeted and informed intercession is unprecedented. When Pierce sends out a red-level prayer alert, a reasonable estimate is that two million intercessors will have received it and acted on it within 24 hours. Internationally, Eagles of God teams function as rapid-deployment, special prayer forces that are ready to move immediately to any part of the world.

A Shift in Theology

Focus on social transformation has also caused many of us to take a second look at some theological presuppositions that until now we have simply assumed. I detail some of our current theological shifts in chapter 9, but here I should mention that the dispensational theology that has caused many of us to expect that God's design is for society to go from bad to worse before Jesus returns is being reexamined. Some who have included specific views of the millennium and the rapture of the Church among their nonnegotiable doctrinal tenets are reconsidering.

What seems to be much more compatible with the goal of expanding the kingdom of God through the transformation of society is a point of view called dominion theology, or Kingdom Now theology. One of the more outspoken advocates of dominion theology has been Bob Weiner, founder of the Maranatha movement. It is true that some unwise applications of Kingdom Now and dominion theology have produced critics; as a result, mid-course corrections have been made. I personally find very important insights in this line of thought.

Let's look, for example, at Bob Weiner's *Take Dominion,* published in the 1980s. He says,

> Through apathy and a lot of bad eschatology we have become fatalists who believe that everything is going to get worse and worse until Jesus finally comes back. But the truth is that God has given His people dominion over this planet, and He expects us to work to see goodness and righteousness established.[2]

Weiner goes back to the creation account to build a theological foundation. He says that God gives us our marching orders in Genesis 1:26 (*NASB*): "Let Us make man in Our image, according to Our likeness; and let them rule over the fish of the sea and over the birds of the sky and over the cattle and over all the earth, and over every creeping thing that creeps on the earth." Weiner comments, "God knew that mankind was going to have dominion, to exercise authority over all the rest of creation. God has not rescinded those orders."[3]

What does this mean for us? Weiner explains,

> We are called to bring the nation itself to Christ. And the nation is made up not only of the people who live there, but of the arts, the sciences, education, law, political systems, the media, business, and so on—in short, every area of life. And if we are to bring the nations to Jesus, our task is to bring every one of those areas of life under His influence and under biblical principles. . . . We need to be getting believers into city government, boards of education, county commissions, and every other area of government. If we are content to withdraw into a corner and not get involved, we are certainly failing in the task God has set before us.[4]

I am fully aware that quite a few leaders of the old wineskin will have their reasons for continuing to oppose dominion theology. I am aware of this because not too long ago, I would have opposed it on the same grounds. However, when I process the kind of things that Bob Weiner and others are saying in light of what I now understand about the kingdom of God, I can only applaud them. This theology helps point the way toward what the Spirit is currently saying to the churches.

A Frustrating Dilemma

So, if church leaders know the direction they are heading and if we have both the correct theology and the practical tools for doing the job, why aren't any of our cities transformed? Some of the top leadership of the Body of Christ have strongly affirmed regional and national transformation as our goal. They have spent huge amounts of time and have invested large sums of money in attempting to push the Church forward down this path. But frustration has begun to set in. Even after 10 years, we cannot point to a single city in the United States that has undergone a sociologically verifiable transformation!

HOPE-GIVING EXAMPLES

The lack of examples of cities that have been transformed is not to imply, however, that social transformation through God's power is impossible. We may not have many examples, but we do have some.

Florence, Italy. Girolamo Savonarola's powerful ministry in Florence, Italy, back in the fifteenth century gives us a historical case study. Here is one description of what happened to the city after Savonarola prayed and prophesied:

> The wicked city government [of Florence] was overthrown, and Savonarola taught the people to set up a democratic form of government. The revival brought tremendous moral change. The people stopped reading vile and worldly books. Merchants made restitution to the people for the excessive profits they had

been making. Hoodlums and street urchins stopped singing sinful songs and began to sing hymns in the streets. Carnivals were forbidden and forsaken.

Huge bonfires were made of worldly books and obscene pictures, masks, and wigs. A great octagonal pyramid of worldly objects was erected in the public square in Florence. It towered in seven stages sixty feet high and 240 feet in circumference. While bells tolled, the people sang hymns and the fire burned.[5]

Let's also look at some current examples.

Uganda. Believers in Uganda attribute the fall of the tyrannical dictator Idi Amin to massive prayer. Since then, the national prayer movement has continued to accelerate strongly. Jackson Senyonga reports that dramatic changes have begun to occur in politics, in the workplace and in the Church. Parliament prays, the police fax prayer requests to judges, and a major bank plays praise music on all 11 floors. In some communities crime is down by 70 percent. Senyonga says, "At one point AIDS in Uganda was at 33.3 percent. The World Health Organization predicted that Uganda's economy would collapse by 1999 or 2000 because there would be only widows and orphans left. So people sought the Lord and prayed. Today, AIDS has dropped to 5 percent."[6]

Fiji. Jack Dennison reports that in Fiji the president, the prime minister and other top government officials have publicly dedicated their nation to Christ. Revivals are turning jails into worship centers. A stream of poisonous water became pure after prayer, fasting and reconciliation. Coral reefs are being suddenly revived after decades of desolation. Fish and crabs are returning to their former breeding grounds.[7]

Almolonga, Guatemala. Nestled in the mountains of Guatemala, the city of Almolonga was a scene of degradation. Drunkenness, family abuse, crime, poverty, violence, drought, disease and natural disasters reigned. Then came the power of God, initially through demonic deliverance. Now over 90 percent of the inhabitants are born again, attractive church buildings dot the landscape, farmers produce world-class vegetables, and prosperity abounds. Not long ago, the last of six jails closed because of the lack of criminals. It has been remodeled into a community center and named the Hall of Honor.[8]

IN UGANDA, DRAMATIC CHANGES HAVE BEGUN TO OCCUR IN POLITICS, IN THE WORKPLACE AND IN THE CHURCH: PARLIAMENT PRAYS, THE POLICE FAX PRAYER REQUESTS TO JUDGES, AND A MAJOR BANK PLAYS PRAISE MUSIC ON ALL 11 FLOORS.

THE EQUATION COMPLETED

While examples such as these provide hope for social transformation, reality forces us to admit that in a huge world, they are all too few and far between. If it is indeed our assignment from God to take dominion over society in His name and to see His kingdom come, we obviously have not been doing a satisfactory job.

How do we explain the fact that the goal of social transformation seems so elusive? There are four possible explanations:

1. Social transformation is an unrealistic goal. It cannot possibly happen.
2. Social transformation is possible, but we have been taking the wrong approach. The spiritual tools we have been using, which I listed above, apparently are not the right tools.
3. We are taking the right approach, but we need to do it more. If 10 years haven't produced the desired results, let's try 10 more.
4. We are taking the right approach, but it is incomplete. Something is missing.

I'll take explanation number four. It seems to me that we have been attempting to replace an established government—designed, empowered and directed by the kingdom of darkness—with a system with inadequate government. This won't work because it takes a government to overthrow a government.

During the 10 years or so that we have been learning about and refining our God-given tools for social transformation, the Body of Christ collectively did not have a clear idea of how the biblical government of the Church should function in the world today. Now that we have entered the Second Apostolic Age, however, we are beginning to understand something about the crucial role of apostles in spiritual government. To complete our equation for social transformation, I believe that we need the presence and active ministry of two kinds of apostles, namely territorial apostles and workplace apostles. If we don't have them, very little will change.

Territorial Apostles

In the last chapter, I told the story of how Julian Watts was recognized by a group of influential pastors as, even though they might not use the term, a territorial apostle in Guildford, England. I believe that was a significant step toward social transformation. I think that one of the mistakes we made in the 1990s was to assume that pastors were the spiritual gatekeepers of the city. This thought appears in my books, as well as in the books of others. We made this mistake because we did not yet understand apostolic government.

According to Scriptures such as 2 Corinthians 10:13-14, apostolic authority is only fully operative within God-assigned apostolic spheres. While these usually are ecclesiastical spheres and sometimes are functional spheres, they also can be territorial spheres. Apostles can be assigned geographical areas, such as cities, as their base of operation. I would hypothesize that every city with a significant Christian presence will already have territorial apostles placed by God in its midst. If this is the case, the leaders of the life-giving churches in that city only need to identify, publicly recognize, empower and submit to the divine authority that they have been given. When they do, the true apostolic gatekeepers of the city will be in place, and the territorial government of the Church will be established.

Workplace Apostles

I do not need to repeat what I said in chapter 4 about apostles in the extended Church, also known as the workplace. In this context, however, I will contend that until these apostles are recognized and properly authorized by church leaders in the city, social transformation will continue to be delayed.

I like the way that Os Hillman addresses this issue. He says,

> [The workplace] is where real transformation can take place, because the workplace is where authority is in the cities. We thought we could change cities through pastors and church leaders and prayer walks. We now need to equip and affirm the apostles, prophets, teachers, evangelists, and pastors in the workplace.[9]

It wouldn't be surprising if, as we move forward in mobilizing workplace apostles, we discover that more of them have been assigned by God to the role of territorial apostles than to nuclear Church apostles. If this is true, we can clearly see that we cannot get on with the task of social transformation properly until workplace apostles are set into place as a vital part of the territorial government of the Church.

THE RELEASE OF WEALTH

Not only will the transformation of society require prayer, spiritual warfare and apostolic leadership, but it will also require money. Since sometime around 1992, recognized prophets have been hearing that God is poised to release unprecedented amounts of wealth for the expansion of

His kingdom. When this wealth is released, the funding that we now have access to will look like pocket change. These prophecies, which appear to be quite authentic, have been given for over 10 years, but the transference of wealth has not yet taken place. Why?

I think that timing is the reason. First, it seems reasonable that God will entrust the Body of Christ with this wealth only after the biblical government of the Church is in place. This happened, according to our calculations, in 2001. Still, the release has not come.

Second, perhaps God is waiting for the workplace apostles to be set in their proper place. Without them and the expertise that they bring to the table, it could well be that this enormous amount of wealth would soon go down a black hole.

THE FOUR LINKS

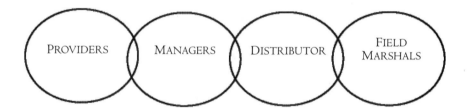

There are four necessary links in the chain of transference of wealth: providers, managers, distributors and field marshals. The goal of the process is to get funds from the providers to the field marshals. The providers are people who have the funds under their control. It doesn't really matter whether they are Christians or non-Christians. The Israelites, for example, were financed by the wealth of the pagan Egyptians. The managers are those who have the skills to handle large sums of money so that, rather than going down a black hole, the money generates a steady cash flow for the kingdom of God. The distributors are networked with the field marshals, to whom they transmit the funds. The field marshals direct the work on the front lines to evangelize, plant churches, care for the poor and needy, and transform society.

I believe that the providers and the field marshals are largely in place. God would not promise the money through the prophets if He did not know that it was available and who controlled it. And around the world we already have identified large numbers of skilled, experienced, trustworthy apostles who know how to use money wisely in extending the kingdom of God. Those are the first and last links in the chain.

We are weak, however, in the middle two links: managers and distributors. Managers undoubtedly would be drawn from workplace apostles. These are individuals who, unlike most nuclear Church apostles, have professional skills in handling large sums of money in the marketplace. But while extended Church apostles may know how to manage the money, most have limited knowledge of how to spend it. This is where the distributors—mostly nuclear Church apostles, it seems to me—come in. They are the ones who have broad relationships with the field marshals, who in turn can most effectively use the funds for the glory of God.

THE EFFECTS OF OBEDIENCE

Having said this, I need to add a caveat. Please do not assume that there is an automatic cause-and-effect relationship between having this chain in place and a society's being transformed. The transformation of society will only occur if God's people are willing to hear the voice of God and obey Him. Instead of a simple cause and effect, let's admit that there is also an underlying "if . . . then," as we find in 2 Chron. 7:14 (emphasis added): "*If* My people who are called by My name will humble themselves, and pray and seek My face, and turn from their wicked ways, *then* I will hear from heaven, and will forgive their sin and heal their land."

A NEW APOSTOLIC DIRECTION

Our view of the kingdom of God has taken us beyond just the expansion of the Church to God's heart desire for the transformation of society. He literally wants His kingdom to come and His will to be done on Earth as it is in heaven. This is truly apostolic thinking.

CHAPTER SEVEN

FROM A TOLERANCE OF THE KINGDOM OF SATAN TO AN INVASION OF THE KINGDOM OF SATAN

BEFORE THE 1990S, THERE WAS HARDLY A PASTOR IN AMERICA WHO HAD TAKEN A COURSE IN SEMINARY OR BIBLE COLLEGE ON SPIRITUAL WARFARE. IT WOULDN'T HAVE OCCURRED TO MOST ORDINATION COUNCILS TO ASK CANDIDATES FOR THE MINISTRY TO EXPLAIN THEIR VIEWS ABOUT SPIRITUAL WARFARE AND TO DESCRIBE THEIR EXPERIENCES IN CASTING OUT DEMONS. MOST DENOMINATIONS DID NOT EXPECT THEIR CENTERS OF THEOLOGICAL EDUCATION TO CONCENTRATE SIGNIFICANT ACADEMIC ACTIVITY ON THE NATURE OF THE INVISIBLE WORLD OF DARKNESS.

I can testify to this situation in America firsthand for two reasons: First, in the process of earning four graduate degrees in religion, I never encountered a single course offering on the subject. Second, when years later I joined the faculty of one of America's most respected seminaries, spiritual warfare had never even been suggested as a part of the curriculum for training clergy.

JESUS AND SPIRITUAL WARFARE

Looking back from the perspective of the Second Apostolic Age, the previous lack of emphasis on spiritual warfare seems very strange, especially when we take Jesus' point of view into account. The Gospels make it very clear that confronting demonic powers was not peripheral to Jesus' thinking; it was central. Jesus seemingly never contemplated a method of spreading the message of the kingdom of God without including demonic deliverance.

For example, when Jesus sent out the 12 apostles, He gave them "power over unclean spirits, to cast them out" (Matt. 10:1). Later, Jesus sent out a group of 70 with the same mandate. When they returned, they expressed their astonishment by reporting, "Lord, even the demons are subject to us in Your name" (Luke 10:17). Before He left the earth, Jesus made the following statement: "These signs will follow those who believe: In My name they will cast out demons" (Mark 16:17).

Jesus saw evangelism as a literal invasion of the kingdom of Satan. To invade means to enter forcefully, to confront with a hostile intent, to intrude upon, to attempt to take possession. In other words, an invasion follows a declaration of war. When Jesus gave Paul his evangelistic assignment on the Damascus road, Paul's commission was to go to the nations "to turn them from darkness to light, and from the power of Satan to God" (Acts 26:18). I have never heard of Satan giving up anyone in his power without a fight. He will assign every demon possible to prevent the spread of the gospel. That is why Jesus routinely empowered His disciples to cast out demons in His name.

SEMINARY AND SPIRITUAL WARFARE

For most of my professional life I have been an academician, trying to play by the rules of the academic community. I must say that one of the rules I never quite understood was academic tenure, the rule that prevents professors, once they reach a certain point in their career, from being fired. But even though I may not have understood or agreed with the rationale behind academic tenure, I was very grateful for it when my job became threatened for introducing spiritual warfare into the curriculum of a respected seminary.

Let me explain.

From Cessationism to Power Ministries

I began my ministry career as a convinced cessationist. This means that I believed that what we now call the charismatic gifts were in effect during the first century or so of Church history but that when the apostolic age ended and the canon of Scripture was completed, they ceased. This caused me to regard Pentecostals and charismatics as the lunatic fringe of Christianity. I wanted as little to do with them as possible.

However, my paradigm began to shift in the late 1960s when I studied church growth under Donald McGavran. I could not deny the fact that the healthiest, most vigorously growing churches in Latin America, where I was then serving as a field missionary, were the Pentecostal churches. Since God's hand of blessing was clearly visible in the Pentecostal churches around me, I was forced to conclude that there might be some validity in their beliefs and practices.

The major human influence in this paradigm shift was John Wimber, founder of the Vineyard movement. I left Bolivia and joined a seminary faculty where I taught church growth. It was there that John Wimber helped me understand how even non-Pentecostal churches could minister in the spiritual gifts that we thought had gone out of use almost 2,000 years ago. Wimber and I began teaching courses on how supernatural signs and wonders have helped churches grow. I turned into an outspoken advocate of power ministries and I even wrote a book about them, *Look Out! The Pentecostals Are Coming* (Creation House).

As might be expected, the courses on signs and wonders produced considerable discomfort among certain of my faculty colleagues who were accustomed to teaching cessationism. That caused a number of serious problems for me. But it was a little later, when I began introducing courses on spiritual warfare, that the crisis relating to my academic tenure erupted.

From a Skirmish to a War

The courses on signs and wonders recognized that ministries of healing and casting out demons constituted an invasion of the kingdom of Satan. However, as I look back now, I perceive that my critics must have regarded the content of these courses as relatively minor issues. It was only when I began advocating overt confrontation with the high-ranking principalities and powers of darkness that the scenario seemed to escalate to an all-out war.

The process began in the historic Congress on World Evangelization, commonly referred to as Lausanne II. The Lausanne Committee for World Evangelization (LCWE) had invited 4,500 leaders from all over the world to gather in Manila in 1989. At that event, no fewer than five speakers addressed a topic heretofore absent from the radar screens of the majority of delegates, namely the subject of territorial spirits. I happened to be one of the five. We suggested that the Church would do well to implement proactively what Paul describes as "[wrestling] against principalities, against powers, against the rulers of the darkness of this age, against spiritual hosts of wickedness in the heavenly places" (Eph. 6:12). We felt that such "air war" was necessary to pave the way for the ground troops of evangelists, church planters and pastors to reach the unreached peoples of the world.

> "AIR WAR" AGAINST THE SPIRITUAL HOSTS OF WICKEDNESS IN THE HEAVENLY REALMS IS NECESSARY TO PAVE THE WAY FOR THE GROUND TROOPS OF EVANGELISTS, CHURCH PLANTERS AND PASTORS TO REACH THE UNREACHED PEOPLES OF THE WORLD.

Some of these speakers postulated that there might be demonic principalities assigned by Satan to keep certain geographic territories in spiritual darkness. Spirits named in the book of Daniel, such as the prince of Persia and the prince of Greece (see Dan. 10:20), could be seen as prototypes of similar satanic activities today. If this were the case, such principalities of evil could turn out to be major deterrents to effective evangelism in certain regions. Many left asking, "Has God given us the authority and the mandate to confront and engage these obstacles to the spread of the Gospel?"

Before I left Manila, I sensed that God was whispering to me, "My son, I want you to take leadership in the area of territorial spirits." I was so sure that I had heard the voice of God that I immediately began to take three steps toward moving into what was for me a previously unexplored field.

From Researcher to Teacher

Since I was a scholar, my first step was to do extensive research in an attempt to uncover material in which others had addressed this subject. To my surprise, I found quite a bit. I collected the best of this material and published it in a book that was released as *Engaging the Enemy* (Regal Books) in the United States and as *Territorial Spirits* (Sovereign World) in the United Kingdom. Well-known figures such as Jack Hayford, David Yonggi Cho, John Dawson, Roger Forster, Ed Silvoso and Michael Green were among the 19 contributors.

My second step was to convene a think tank so that leaders who had insights into what we were then calling territorial spirits could sit down together, learn from each other and form a critical mass of leaders to communicate these relatively new ideas to the body of Christ. The group of 25 or so met several times and adopted the name "The Spiritual Warfare Network" (SWN). It was then, in the early 1990s, that we agreed on the terminology: "ground-level spiritual warfare" (casting out demons), "occult-level spiritual warfare" (confronting organized evil forces, such as satanism, witchcraft, New Age, Freemasonry and Eastern religions) and "strategic-level spiritual warfare" (engaging high-ranking principalities of darkness, such as territorial spirits).

The third step was to begin teaching this rather innovative material in my seminary classes. Earlier courses in signs and wonders had stretched the boundaries of faculty comfort zones considerably, but this corollary introducing the possibility of dealing directly with something like a spirit of Greece was too much for many theologians. They did not want their students exposed to what they considered to be outlandish ideas. They then relegated me to the lunatic fringe.

The upshot was that the faculty senate called me in for what amounted to a heresy trial. They succeeded in humiliating me, but they did not succeed in having me dismissed. Why? There were only three grounds on which a tenured professor could be dismissed: immorality, financial dishonesty and heresy. No questions were raised about my morality or financial integrity. However, although many senate members thought I had crossed the line into heresy, none of them could prove that I had violated any of the items found in the seminary's statement of faith. Fortunately for me, the framers of the seminary's creed must not have believed that statements concerning demons or principalities or the person and work of Satan or the invisible world of darkness or spiritual warfare or deliverance merited a place in a respectable seminary's catalog.

A DISTINCTIVE FEATURE OF A GENUINE APOSTLE IS TO LEAD THE CHURCH INTO AN INVASION OF SATAN'S KINGDOM.

THE CHRISTIAN ANTIWAR MOVEMENT

One of the things that I discovered through this process was the surprising fact that a subtle antiwar movement exists within the Church. This is not something new. In fact, it undoubtedly dates back at least to the Enlightenment of the eighteenth century. I recall my seminary professors having a wry smile on their faces and a knowing look in their eyes when they described the famous incident of Martin Luther throwing an inkwell at a demon in his study. Luther was pre-Enlightenment, in their thinking; so through no fault of his, he had been deprived of the benefits emerging from the age of human reason that had molded the minds of my teachers. On that basis, they cut Luther some slack.

A prominent theme that runs through this book has to do with the corporate spirit of religion. I will continue to repeat that the major assignment this spirit has received is to prevent God's people from moving into the new times and seasons that God desires for the Church. The spirit of religion is a preserver of the status quo. It devises ways and means to make the old wineskin so appealing that Christian leaders are either oblivious to God's new wineskin or they actively oppose it.

Promoting a Christian antiwar movement would be natural for the corporate spirit of religion. The Second Apostolic Age is characterized by an increased desire on the part of God's people to engage in spiritual warfare. This would be expected since the foundation of the Church, namely apostles and prophets (see Eph. 2:20), has now come into place. A distinctive feature of the nature of a genuine apostle is to lead the Church into an invasion of Satan's kingdom. Naturally, apostles will be opposed by those who choose to become Christian pacifists.

WARRIOR-APOSTLES

To help us understand the mentality of leaders of the Second Apostolic Age, let's hear directly from three of our more prominent contemporary apostles.

John Eckhardt of Crusaders Ministries in Chicago says,

> Apostolic ministry is a ministry of warfare. It entails commanding, mobilizing, rallying and gathering the army of God to challenge and pull down the strongholds of the enemy. The apostolic invades new territories and breaks through. It has the ability to go first. It is the first to encounter the spiritual resistance of the powers of darkness and the first to penetrate the barriers they erect.[1]

Chuck Pierce, a respected prophet-apostle, says,

> Through the resurgence of the prophetic and the apostolic, we are destroying the demonic structures in the second heaven that have been holding both the Church and the unsaved world captive. God is teaching us methods and strategies that will rip the blinders off the eyes of whole territories of people. This new warring anointing will cause us to reap a great and bountiful harvest of souls![2]

John Kelly, a leader of the International Coalition of Apostles (ICA), says,

> Warfare is the number-one role of the apostle. Prophets will woo you with the Word of the Lord; teachers will educate you; pastors will help you through your problems and hurts; evangelists will get folks saved; but it is the apostle who will declare war on the enemy and lead the Church to war. The apostle is the one who will unify the Church into a fighting force. The apostle is the one who will bring all past and present truth and every past and present move of God to bear against the enemy.[3]

If what Eckhardt, Pierce and Kelly say is true, it is easy to see why the spirit of religion would be giving a high priority to promoting a Christian antiwar movement. I think it is safe to postulate that the overt threat to the activities of Satan and his demonic forces is far greater now than it has been for a long, long time.

The spirit of religion has a fairly easy job of promoting peace because peace is so appealing. War is extremely uncomfortable. Who wants war? The antiwar movement cuts across the boundaries between Pentecostals and non-Pentecostals. There are some who believe that Satan and demons are real, but that we should ignore them as much as possible. Their attitude is "If we don't bother them, they won't bother us." This statement is true to a degree, simply because tolerating the kingdom of Satan plays directly into the hands of the spirit of religion. Why should the devil bother those who are, albeit inadvertently, helping to protect his kingdom from possible invasion?

Dale Sides, another recognized apostolic leader, reflects the irritation that most apostles feel concerning the antiwar movement. He says,

> I continually have people, who were once engaged in the battle against the unseen hosts of Satan, come to me with a long face and a defeated look saying, "I heard that I do not have authority

against principalities and powers, and I read in a book that if I get involved in this then I will get hurt."[4]

"Unfortunately," Sides continues, "the writer heard a couple of horror stories. He is doing the same damage to the Church as the ten spies did in Joshua's time, when they caused the children of Israel to be afraid."[5]

IT TAKES WAR TO MAKE PEACE.

THE VALUE OF WAR

Peace is ideal, but it takes war to make peace. I have been blessed by living most of my life in peace. What allowed this to happen was the last war officially declared by the United States Congress: World War II. I was a teenager during World War II, so I know what real war is—and I don't like it. But I do like the 50 years of peace that it produced.

Some younger people who might not remember World War II are likely to remember the Vietnam War, a war that America lost. There were some major differences between the two wars. One was the fact that Congress never declared war on Vietnam. Consequently, it was at best a halfhearted effort. Another was the spate of antiwar movements across the country during the Vietnam War. I don't recall a single antiwar movement during World War II. At that time, it never occurred to us to criticize our leaders or to complain about the personal sacrifices that war required: Sugar was rationed; we needed stamps to buy shoes; we couldn't fill our gas tanks or take pleasure drives; we saved paper and scrap metal; we bought savings bonds; and we said goodbye to our relatives, many of whom we never saw again.

Jesus is known as the Prince of Peace. However, look at the words that He spoke: "Do not think that I came to bring peace on earth. I did not come to bring peace but a sword" (Matt. 10:34). One reason He said this was that he had come to Earth in order to invade the kingdom of Satan. Jesus said, "From the days of John the Baptist until now, the kingdom of heaven has been forcefully advancing, and forceful men lay hold of it" (Matt. 11:12, *NIV*). Apostles take Jesus' words literally, and they take seriously their role as generals, leading the Church into war. They realize that peace eventually will come, but not without war.

THREE FRONTS OF THE ANTIWAR MOVEMENT

As I see it, the corporate spirit of religion is currently attempting to orchestrate the Christian antiwar movement on three fronts.

The first front relates to a large number of church leaders who do not believe that Satan or demons actually exist. The concept of demons, in their minds, might be useful to describe evil influences produced by unrighteous people or unjust social structures, but they are not to be regarded as personalities who could be confronted, engaged and dealt with. Naturally, the spirit of religion desires to maintain this status quo, and the task is relatively easy. Among this group, we find a relatively low view of biblical authority and a typical indifference to the person and work of the Holy Spirit. These leaders see little need to declare war against a figment of the imagination.

The second front is directed toward Bible believers who have concluded that Jesus has given us only limited authority in the invisible world. To them, Satan is real and demons are real. They believe in spiritual warfare, but only to a point. Yes, we can and should cast demons out of individuals who are tormented. But we have no authority above that ground level. We step out of bounds if we confront principalities or powers or territorial spirits. If we are foolish enough to attempt that, they contend that we do so at our own risk, with a high chance that we will end up as casualties because God has not promised us His protection in that arena. This would not be regarded as a total antiwar movement; more accurately it would constitute an antistrategic-level spiritual warfare movement. In this case, the corporate spirit of religion, in all likelihood, would put up with some demonic expulsion as long as it could prevent believers from taking authority on higher levels; it would prevent them from taking authority by transmitting to them a spirit of fear.

The spirit of religion's strategy on the third front attempts to neutralize God's forces by convincing some that Christian believers cannot be demonized. Even though this contradicts the position and practice of today's most respected deliverance ministers, antiwar proponents maintain their outspoken opposition to ministry that is directed toward freeing believers from bondage by casting out demons. For example, the members of the International Society of Deliverance Ministers (ISDM) have no doubt at all that many believers, in fact, need deliverance, and they spend a good part of their time providing it for them when necessary. Many consider Simon the Sorcerer a case in point. He was a baptized believer, but he was also "*bound* by iniquity" (Acts 8:23, emphasis added). When skilled deliverance ministers read this somewhat technical language, they intuitively regard Simon as a typical candidate for deliverance. And they also go on to hope that his request for prayer (see v. 24) eventually led to his freedom, although Luke's account does not follow through and confirm that particular point for us.

SCRIPTURAL GUIDELINES FOR WARFARE

War, specifically biblical spiritual warfare, is a characteristic of the Second Apostolic Age. Now that apostles are in place, the Spirit is strongly speaking to the churches about becoming more aggressive. It is time to go to war! We are not to *tolerate* the kingdom of Satan; we are to *invade* it. The antiwar movement is a relic of the old wineskin, which the spirit of religion is actively attempting to preserve. We must not allow this to happen. Here are some scriptural guidelines that will help us see the picture clearly enough to keep us at arm's length from the Christian antiwar movement.

Our Mandate

Our mandate is clear. Jesus left heaven and came to Earth "to seek and to save that which was lost" (Luke 19:10). When He went back to heaven, He left us with the mandate to preach the gospel to every creature (see Mark 16:15) and to make disciples of all nations (see Matt. 28:19-20).

When we preach the gospel, the good news of salvation, to lost people and they do not respond, something is wrong. This is the best news they could ever hear, but when they don't accept it, why not? The Bible is clear: "But even if our gospel is veiled, it is veiled to those who are perishing, *whose minds the god of this age has blinded,* who do not believe, lest the light of the gospel of the glory of Christ, who is the image of God, should shine on them" (2 Cor. 4:3-4, emphasis added).

The "god of this age," a synonym for Satan, is at the root of this. His agenda is the greatest obstacle to the spread of the gospel. Since this is the case, it would not be unreasonable to expect that God would provide us the necessary tools for removing these obstacles that he puts up. Let's do it!

Our Assignment

Our assignment is to attack aggressively. Now is not the time for passivity. Sitting back and hoping against hope that someone else (like God!) may come along and do the job for us will not carry the day. God did not say, "I will evangelize the world." He said, "*You* will evangelize the world."

Our assignment, therefore, is to go into the invisible world for hand-to-hand combat, to "wrestle," as Paul said, making reference to the closest and most intense contact sport in Greco-Roman culture: "For we do not wrestle against flesh and blood, but against principalities, against powers, against the rulers of the darkness of this age, against spiritual hosts of wickedness in the heavenly places" (Eph. 6:12).

Our Weapons

Our weapons come from the arsenal of heaven. The Bible says, "For though we walk in the flesh, we do not war according to the flesh" (2 Cor. 10:3). It is important to recognize that it does not say, "we do not war." Just the opposite. We do war, but we had better not do it in our own strength. Why? "For the weapons of our warfare are not carnal but mighty in God for pulling down strongholds" (2 Cor. 10:4). There can be no doubt that as long as we depend on God's weapons, we have the ways and means to defeat our enemy.

Our Authority

Our authority is unlimited. Here is what Jesus said to His disciples when He sent them out to war: "Behold, I give you authority to trample on serpents and scorpions, and over all the power of the enemy, and nothing shall by any means hurt you" (Luke 10:19). The reference to serpents and scorpions is not to be taken as literal language. They are figures of speech meaning spiritual forces of darkness. Jesus did not say that He gives His disciples authority over *some* of the power of the enemy. We are not limited to ground-level spiritual warfare. If we take His words at face value, we will conclude that we have authority over *all* the power of the enemy—at the occult level and the strategic level as well as at the ground level.

Our Responsibility

Our responsibility is to confront high-level spirits directly by declaring to them the will of God. God's desire is that "the manifold wisdom of God might be made known by the *church* to the principalities and powers in the heavenly places" (Eph. 3:10, emphasis added). Certain antiwar advocates would have us believe that, while we may command demons to leave individuals, we must not address higher-ranking spiritual beings. However, this Scripture specifically tells us that the Church—those of us who are believers—is expected to declare God's wisdom to principalities and powers.

GENERALS IN GOD'S ARMY

Some who read this will observe that these ideas about spiritual warfare, especially on the higher levels, are not prominent in literature throughout the history of the Church. It is not that they are absent; they do appear from time to time, as I have documented elsewhere.[6] However, it is true that such teaching, at least to our knowledge, has never been as prominent and widespread as it is today. That is one reason why most leaders today did not have courses in spiritual warfare in seminary or Bible college, as I mentioned previously. I personally spent some time retracing my own seminary experience and wrote a small book, *Seven Power Principles That I Did Not Learn in Seminary* (Wagner Publications). Since invading the kingdom of Satan is not new to God, why then would the Spirit have waited until only recently to speak to the churches about it?

I think that the answer to this intriguing question lies in the theme of this book, namely the Second Apostolic Age. Apostles are the major figures to whom God has given the role of serving as generals in His army, to use a military term. Consequently, while the Church has always been in a spiritual battle to some degree, it is understandable that God would hesitate to release His armies into higher levels of conflict until His apostolic generals were in place.

A NEW APOSTOLIC DIRECTION

Now that apostles are in place, the kingdom of Satan is in trouble. He may send spirits of religion to try to preserve the status quo. He may convince some believers that they should continue tolerating the kingdom of Satan. He may make the old wineskin seem very appealing. But this is not the direction the Church is taking in the Second Apostolic Age.

We are moving from a tolerance of the kingdom of Satan to an invasion of the kingdom of Satan!

CHAPTER EIGHT

FROM THEOLOGICAL EDUCATION TO EQUIPPING MINISTERS

I WAS RECENTLY TALKING TO A YOUNG MAN WHO HAD GRADUATED FROM THEOLOGICAL SEMINARY YEARS AGO AND WHO IS NOW AN ORDAINED MINISTER. AS HE WAS DISCUSSING HIS SEMINARY TRAINING, HE SAID, "I PAID $8,000 10 YEARS AGO TO LEARN GREEK AND HEBREW, AND NOW THAT I AM IN MINISTRY, I CONSIDER IT A WASTE OF MONEY. I HAVE NEVER FOUND A USE FOR WHAT I WAS TAUGHT." AS SOON AS HE MENTIONED IT, I BEGAN TO THINK BACK TO THOSE ENDLESS HOURS THAT I ALSO SPENT IN LANGUAGE CLASSES. I HATE TO ADMIT IT, BUT A YEAR OR SO AFTER I GRADUATED I COULDN'T EVEN READ THE TITLE ON THE COVER OF THE HEBREW BIBLE!

A SERIOUS CRISIS

What's going on? Are the two of us oddballs? I don't think so. A growing body of evidence points to a serious crisis in the way that Christian leaders are looking at the traditional methodologies supposedly training our people for ordained ministry.

Take, for example, the research that Christian Schwartz of the Institute for Church Development has done on what he calls natural church development. Schwartz holds the distinction of having completed the most comprehensive field study of church growth and health ever recorded. He researched more than 1,000 churches in 32 nations in order to compile his data. Among the many conclusions that Schwartz drew from his research is this rather astounding observation: "Formal theological training has a negative correlation to both church growth and overall quality of churches."[1] Of the highest-quality and fastest-growing churches of these 1,000 churches, only 42 percent of the pastors had graduated from seminary. On the other hand, of the lowest-quality and declining churches, a full 85 percent of the pastors had graduated from seminary.[2]

It goes without saying that these findings are contrary to the assumptions that we have traditionally held. It is a fact that a large number of denominations continue to require a degree from theological seminary to qualify for ordination, and many also require that the degree be from one of their own denominational schools. The reason for this was that denominational leaders simply assumed that they had set in place an educational system that would produce the highest quality pastors and, thereby, that the churches they lead would also be of the highest quality. So far it does not appear that Christian Schwartz's research findings have been seen as a wake-up call for many of them.

As I have mentioned, I serve as a leader of the International Coalition of Apostles (ICA). The ICA is composed of over 350 outstanding leaders of the Apostolic Reformation, all of whom are recognized apostles. What sort of formalized education do these apostles have? To try to answer that question, I did a survey of members. I was not surprised to find that over 60 percent of these apostles have never graduated from seminary or Bible college. This would seem to coincide with what Christian Schwartz has been finding.

FROM HIS COMPREHENSIVE RESEARCH, SCHWARTZ
DREW THIS ASTOUNDING OBSERVATION:
"FORMAL THEOLOGICAL TRAINING
HAS A NEGATIVE CORRELATION TO
BOTH CHURCH GROWTH AND
OVERALL QUALITY OF THE CHURCHES."

GEORGE BARNA'S CONCLUSIONS

George Barna, widely regarded as the premier researcher of church affairs in America, has arrived at similar conclusions. In a privately circulated document describing current research initiatives of the Barna Institute, he reports these significant findings:

Most pastors agree that they were inadequately trained for the job of leading the local church. Yet, seminaries continue to forge ahead, providing much of the same irrelevant (and in some cases misleading and harmful) education that has been their forte for the past century. One response has been churches creating their own ministry education centers to raise up leaders and teachers from within their congregations. Another response has been for churches to hire believers who have secular training and experience in professional fields and allow them to learn the content of ministry realities while they are on the job. There is little doubt that churches are in desperate need of effective leadership as the challenges confronting the Church become more complex, more numerous and more daunting.

But how will those leaders de identified, developed and nurtured for effective ministry leadership? Is there a role for the seminary in the future of the Church? If so, what should the seminary look like and what would its ideal role be? If churches continue to rely on seminaries or some alternative developmental structure to provide them with leaders, it is imperative that the leader training grounds be reshaped. Mere tinkering with a broken system won't provide the answer; creating a holistic, strategic, and intelligently-crafted process is needed.[3]

In a later research project, George Barna tested Christian leaders in America to see if they had a truly biblical worldview. He found that, in terms of education, the pastors least likely to have a biblical worldview are those who graduated from seminary (45 percent). On the other hand, 59 percent of pastors who never attended seminary have a biblical worldview.[4]

The following quote from Aubrey Malphurs, a seminary professor, confirms the inadequate preparation that pastors receive in seminary:

Many seminaries have done a good job of providing future pastors with a knowledge of the Bible, the original languages, church history, and so on. However, they have provided little if any training in the spiritual life, leadership, culture, evangelism, and other practical essentials of ministry.[5]

Fortunately, the Church's "leader training grounds," as Barna puts it, are currently being reshaped as a part of the New Apostolic Reformation. New wineskins, not just patched-up old wineskins, are now beginning to be seen in many of the churches and apostolic networks of the Second Apostolic Age.

Before we look at where we are going, however, let's try to understand where today's traditional theological education came from. How did we get ourselves into the worrisome situation that Christian Schwartz and George Barna describe?

THE ACADEMY MODEL

Let's listen for a moment to one of America's most respected mega-church pastors, Leith Anderson:

> Much theological education is based on the "academy model" of classical European universities. Students are trained to be schol-ars. They are given the tools for research and analysis, and then are trained to be theoretical theologians. . . . The rub comes when the graduates face the realities of parish ministries. There is little time for the more leisurely life of scholarship. People aren't asking for academic alternatives, they are expecting prac-tical answers to life's problems.[6]

Anderson, who has paid his academic dues by earning a doctorate from a traditional seminary, puts his finger on a very significant source of today's problem, namely our European heritage.

An obvious reason for why students are not adequately trained for ministry, then, is the fact that seminaries, by and large, pride themselves on recruiting the purest scholars available for their faculties. Like still begets like. Scholars tend to produce scholars, not hands-on pastors.

Many times over I have heard stories of seminary graduates who fail in their first pastorate and then decide to reenter academia so that they can join seminary faculties in order to teach future pastors.

THE CRITICAL MIND

One of the causes of the dissonance between the seminary classroom and the parish is the high value that scholars typically assign to criticism. Finding something wrong with the Church, with society, with culture and with the opinions of fellow scholars is rewarded by the academy. An unwritten rule for academic book reviews is that the reviewer must point out one or more faults of the book. The seminary in which I teach requires student evaluations of the professor after every course. One of the questions relates to how successful the teacher was to help students develop a critical mind. The subtitle of the respected old-line denominational magazine *The Christian Century* reflects this mindset: "Thinking critically, living faithfully." Sending pastors to parishes with critical minds is like asking baseball players to bat with tennis rackets.

THE MONASTERY MIND-SET

This old wineskin of theological education, in which many of us were trained, can be traced back at least to the Middle Ages in Europe. Although it may be difficult for us to imagine, back then hardly anyone knew how to read and write. The vast majority of Europeans in the Middle Ages were illiterate. It, therefore, became a badge of distinction for a person to be able to read and write.

Among those few who were literate were the Christian monks. Monasteries took their place among the most respected medieval centers of learning. A huge difference between clergy and most laity was that the clergy could read and write. However, they found themselves limited. The language that monks were trained to read and write was the official language of the Church: Latin. In the Middle Ages, the Bible was only available in Latin, not in the vernacular languages of the church members. Therefore, in European society it became axiomatic that the church leaders, the clergy, were found among the best-educated individuals in the community. The conclusion: Clergy equals academic attainment.

The monasteries created the mind-set in the Church through the years that respectable clergy should be better educated than lay church members in general. This idea was not changed in the Protestant Reformation, although universities rather than monasteries soon became the standard incubator for Protestant clergy. The concept of academy then took root, resurrecting the term that Plato used to designate his philosophical school. This is where we get our word "academic."

THE MONASTERIES CREATED THE MIND-SET IN THE CHURCH THAT RESPECTABLE CLERGY SHOULD BE BETTER EDUCATED THAN LAY CHURCH MEMBERS.

While there were academies for different branches of learning, the one that had to do with educating clergy became known as the theological academy. Members of the theological academy were those scholars trained in church history, biblical studies, philosophy, theology and church polity; this training was seen as qualifying these scholars to educate young people desiring ordination.

In America, while some free spirits, such as the early Methodists, broke tradition, the presumption that academic theological education was a prerequisite for the pastorate prevailed. For example, our oldest American university, Harvard (first called Harvard College), was founded exclusively to educate men for the Christian ministry, as was Yale. Here is how President Thomas Clap of Yale defined a college: "Colleges are Societies of Ministers for training up Persons for the Work of the Ministry."[7]

MINISTERS AS INTELLECTUAL LEADERS

Up until the twentieth century, Christian ministers, along with doctors and lawyers, were regarded to be among the best-educated Americans. Particularly in rural areas but also in cities, it was generally assumed that ministers should be intellectual leaders in their communities, and more frequently than not, they were.

The picture began to change in the twentieth century, due primarily to two simultaneous social phenomena. One was the urbanization of America, and the other was the rapid escalation of opportunities for schooling—a direct corollary, by the way, of economic prosperity. For example, my father was considered well-educated with one year of college. In my generation, the same status required a full college degree. In my children's generation, graduate school became necessary.

The assumption of the Church was that pastors needed to keep ahead of the rest educationally. Therefore graduate theological seminaries became the norm for training ministers. It was almost inconceivable to many that a pastor could effectively serve a flock of individuals who had achieved higher academic levels.

The Monastic Model

However, theological seminaries persisted in looking to the monasteries as their model. Curricula and faculties remained essentially the same, offering education primarily in Church history, biblical studies, philosophy, theology and church polity. Scholarship, particularly critical scholarship, ruled. The dress code at official functions was the medieval academic regalia. Even terminology was adapted to monastic life. For example, at Fuller Theological Seminary, where I studied and still teach, the cafeteria was to be known as the refectory, and the outdoor patio was the garth, referring to the courtyard enclosed by a cloister in the typical monastery. On the wall of my study I have diplomas certifying the three graduate degrees that I received from seminaries: two from Fuller and one from Princeton. Remarkably, I cannot read any of them. All three are in Latin!

The assumption on the part of Christian denominational leaders and educational power brokers was that academic theological seminaries, rooted in the monasteries, were essential for maintaining a well-educated clergy and for protecting the Church from the incursion of heresy. Graduate study, it was supposed, produces the best ministers. Enter Christian Schwartz and his research. Could it be that those suppositions are flawed?

Heresy

Speaking of heresy, it is notable that through the years, the premier center of Protestant intellectual theological development was Western Europe, particularly Germany, German-speaking Switzerland and the Netherlands. Those who applied for the best chairs in the most prestigious theological seminaries in America did themselves well to have advanced degrees from these nations on their résumés. An interesting question arises: Did this learning protect the Protestant churches of these nations from heresy? Far from it. Some of the most unbiblical theology in all of Church history emerged from these prestigious European centers of scholarship, and the Protestant Church in each of the three nations I have named is currently regarded by the population as socially irrelevant and is just this side of extinction.

A BROKEN SYSTEM

Church leaders in the Second Apostolic Age are saying that enough is enough. But they are still in the minority in America. The majority are persisting in what George Barna calls "mere tinkering with a broken system."[8] Here again is the tension that I have described in the other chapters. Should we attempt to pour new wine into old wineskins, or should we take the risk of moving forward into new wineskins?

Predictably, if my hypotheses concerning the spirit of religion are correct, the corporate spirit of religion would undoubtedly have received an assignment to work among those who control the theological education establishment, attempting to make them think that maintaining the status quo is the will of God. Members of the academic community have a relatively leisurely and comfortable lifestyle. They don't punch time clocks. They are rarely subject to performance reviews. They enjoy the job security of academic tenure. Whereas law schools, business schools and medical schools are frequently evaluated by the general public according to the quality of their graduates, this does not usually happen with a theological seminary. Consequently, a spirit of religion assigned to maintain the status quo of theological education would have a relatively easy task.

THE CHANGING FOCUS

How is the focus changing in the Second Apostolic Age?

As I have mentioned several times, Ephesians 4, where Paul describes how Jesus, at His ascension, provided the Church that He left behind with apostles, prophets, evangelists, pastors and teachers, has become a fundamental biblical text for leaders of the Second Apostolic Age. In the immediate biblical passage, it is notable that one and only one task of these leaders is mentioned: "the equipping of the saints for the work of the ministry, for the edifying of the body of Christ" (Eph. 4:12).

Equipping the saints for the work of the ministry has several important implications if we take it at face value. One of them is that the people who need to be equipped are "the saints," or all the people of God. Another is that each individual saint has been assigned a ministry that requires a particular kind of resourcing. A third is that "equipping" means to provide whatever resources might be necessary to enable persons to do what is required of them.

Equipping the saints, therefore, will certainly include schooling, but it includes much more. It encompasses a much broader scope than most traditional seminaries and Bible schools have been able to provide. It certainly needs to go beyond the standard curriculum of theological education. It wasn't too long ago, for example, that throughout the seminaries where many of us were teaching, an energetic debate was being carried on as to whether a seminary was or was not responsible for the spiritual life and character of its students. As I recall, the outcome was more or less a standoff. At least half of the professors believed that focusing on the students' heads, to the exclusion of their hearts, was sufficient.

This is where the title of this chapter comes into play: "From Theological Education to Equipping Ministers." Apostolic leaders are no longer satisfied with a monastic model designed to educate a few clergy on a higher academic level than most laity. Their desire is a broad, open, fluid system that will equip the saints for the work of the ministry. In short, whatever training centers emerge in the Second Apostolic Age will inevitably be evaluated on their ability to equip ministers, nothing more and nothing less.

The focus of traditional theological education is on the quality of the academic institution. The focus of equipping ministers is on the quality of the student, or the saint. The old wineskin presumed that if we have the right curriculum, the right faculty and the right scholarly environment, we will succeed in educating the highest-quality clergy. On the other hand, the new wineskin recognizes the fact that we have so many different saints and so many different ministries that no one institution or no one educational style could possibly suffice. Any number of creative training programs would need to be tailor-made to fit diverse ministry challenges.

ORDINATION

One of the key issues relates to ordination. It has become customary in our society to recognize certain individuals as ordained ministers. In fact our federal government, through the IRS, favors ordained ministers through a number of tax advantages. The presumption of the general public is that one must be ordained in order to lead a local congregation.

How, then, does a person gain entrance to the category of ordained minister? Although there have been exceptions, at least in churches of European-American heritage, the first step toward ordination would be seen as proper education. While details might vary from denomination to denomination, most would expect their ordinands (the technical term for candidates for ordination) to be adequately schooled in Church history, biblical studies, philosophy, theology and church polity. This definition of a proper education has given traditional theological education a virtual corner on the market for ordination training.

A New View of Ordination

However, individuals, congregations and groupings of churches that have entered the Second Apostolic Age are now questioning the basic presuppositions underlying old-wineskin concepts of ordination. As a starter, they argue that the New Testament does not even distinguish between ordained and unordained ministry. In their understanding, all the saints—not just selected clergy—are to do the work of the ministry; therefore, all should be regarded as bona fide ministers.

ALL THE SAINTS—NOT JUST SELECTED CLERGY—
ARE TO DO THE WORK OF THE MINISTRY.

Second, they point out that the New Testament requirements for the few specified church-leadership positions such as deacons, elders and bishops do not include things like Church history, biblical studies, philosophy, theology and church polity. The biblical requirements invariably have more to do with character than with educational attainments.

For example, when I was ordained back in the 1950s, my examining committee, made up of ordained ministers, thoroughly questioned me on biblical, theological and historical concepts. They were simply following the standard procedure of the day. Curiously, I do not recall them requiring me to assure them that I was blameless, the husband of one wife, apt to teach, a good ruler of my household, having my children in subjection, not a novice and the recipient of a good report among those who were outside, just to select a few of the biblical leadership requirements from 1 Timothy 3. Such things, in fact, had not been an explicit part of my seminary education. In checking out my three-year MDiv curriculum, I find that I took and passed 50 different courses, none of which directly related to the character requirements of 1 Timothy 3. Granted, one of the 50 courses was Christian Ethics, but as I recall, it focused more on the philosophy of ethics than on applying ethical principles to my personal life.

Implications of Ordination

To understand how and why these changes are taking place in the Second Apostolic Age, we need to understand exactly what ordination implies. In my view, ordination is simply the recognition by the Body of Christ that an individual has certain spiritual gifts relating to church leadership and is authorized to use them in appropriate ministry. The most common application of this is our custom of ordaining pastors of our local churches. Those who do the ordaining do not presume to give the gift of pastor; God gives that gift. Ordination, however, sets those with the recognized *gift* of pastor into the *office* of pastor. This opens doors for ministry that otherwise might remain closed.

Obviously, ordination is not to be restricted to the office of pastor. It equally applies to the offices of apostle, prophet, evangelist and teacher, just to name a few. Some would add intercessor or deacon or parachurch ministry leader or deliverance minister or worship leader or counselor or others. There are those who advocate ordaining individuals who fulfill godly leadership roles in the workplace (extended Church), not necessarily limiting ordination to nuclear Church leaders, as we have ordinarily done.

With this broadened concept of ordination and ministry, demands for training become substantially different in the new wineskin. Academic attainment is no longer the first hurdle to jump, although academic degrees do not necessarily disqualify a person. Experience, maturity and character become more important than formal learning. One rather obvious ripple effect of this new-wineskin thinking is that the traditional seminary and Bible school will no longer have a corner on the market for training ordinands.

THE INCUBATOR FOR CHURCH LEADERS

In fact, the congregation is now replacing seminaries as the primary incubator for church leaders. Parish consultant Lyle Schaller saw this change coming as early as 1988:

> Congregations, not academic institutions, once again are becoming the primary place for training program staff members for large congregations. This is consistent and compatible, but farther advanced than a parallel trend, that is for large churches to replace theological seminaries as the primary source for clergy.[9]

It is becoming more and more common for senior pastors to invite church members, whose character and spiritual gifts they have observed in action over a period of time, to fill staff positions, rather than asking for résumés from seminaries as they used to do.

Most pastors in the Second Apostolic Age have no hesitation in ordaining these gifted individuals, even though the individuals hold no degree from seminary or Bible college. The ordinands are not examined on Church history, biblical studies, philosophy, theology or church polity. They are ordained on the basis of their recognized anointing of God for the ministry to which they have been called.

It almost goes without saying that the reality of what I have just described completely changes the picture for institutions designed for training ministers. The issue no longer is how well church leaders are educated theologically; rather, it is how well they are equipped for ministry.

It might bear mention that, at least at the time of this writing, none of the senior pastors of the five largest megachurches in America, all with attendance of over 18,000, have seminary degrees. And many other notable leaders, such as Bill Hybels of Willow Creek Community Church, Chuck Colson of Prison Fellowship, Bill McCartney, founder of Promise Keepers, James Dobson of Focus on the Family, Ted Haggard of the National Association of Evangelicals and the late Bill Bright of Campus Crusade, just to name a few, never found it necessary to pursue seminary degrees.

Although this book is mostly focused on the American church scene, I think it would be worthwhile to take a moment to look at the Third World, specifically at China. For several years, I have been saying in public that I foresee that the nation that will be sending more missionaries to other nations in the year 2010 will be Brazil and that Brazil will be replaced by China in 2025. It is only recently that we Americans have become aware that for over 20 years Chinese Christian leaders have envisioned the Back to Jerusalem movement, which has the goal of sending 100,000 Chinese missionaries to evangelize all the nations and people groups between China and Jerusalem. This movement has actually begun, with hundreds of Chinese missionaries on the field and thousands more in training.

Listen to the comment of Paul Hattaway, one of the premier researchers of the Back to Jerusalem movement:

> According to normal Western missionary methods, these workers were unqualified. None had ever attended a seminary and most would think that a theological degree is something found on a thermometer! Yet they had received training from God that is far more important than what can be learned in a classroom, an experiential training in the furnace of affliction.[10]

Might we be observing, through this, a wave of the future?

NEW FORMS OF CHURCH

To complicate matters even further, new forms of church—not on the radar screen of most seminaries and Bible schools—are becoming an increasingly significant part of our American ecclesiastical landscape. By and large, seminary faculties presume that the typical graduate will pastor a congregation of under 200 members, which is affiliated with a recognized denomination (very frequently the denomination that has sponsored the seminary). Consequently, most seminary graduates end up pastoring small, traditional local churches.

But things are changing. While traditional local churches will undoubtedly continue to provide the normal places of worship for most American believers, they will no longer be the only option. Some of the forms that other options for churches are taking include but are not limited to:

- **House churches.** These are churches that follow the New Testament pattern of meeting in homes. Ordinarily they are the size that can fit into a living room. The members are free to participate in the services as they feel God is leading them. They avoid clergy-laity distinctions in practice as well as in theory. Strong pastoral leadership is not required. Pastoral care is done by the group, not by designated individuals. Every member is considered a minister.
- **Corporate churches.** Now that the validity of the extended Church is being more widely affirmed, some workplace leaders, aware that many of their colleagues are open to God, are facing the reality that persuading them to attend a traditional church on Sunday may not be the best way to reach them. A number of them are experimenting with establishing corporate churches in the workplace environment. These are not Bible studies or prayer groups but are small congregations that typically meet one evening a week. For many of those who attend, this is the church where they regularly worship, study the Word, pay their tithe, minister to others and receive ministry.

· **Privatization of religion.** American sociologists of religion, led by Robert Bellah, have been observing the privatization of religion since at least 1985.[11] Others call it individualization.[12] An observer from New Zealand uses the term "out-of-church Christians."[13] He estimates that in the city of Auckland alone there are tens of thousands of "the most committed kind of Christians . . . [who] have grown tired of 'playing the game' inside our church system and have opted out." After these Christians had tried many different churches, "it just seemed easier to stay at home with God." Back in America, a Gallup poll has found that 76 percent of Americans agree that a person can be a good Christian or Jew without attending a church or synagogue.[14]

My purpose here is not so much to detail the inner workings of these new forms of church but rather to point out the obvious: New forms of church will require new forms of leadership training.

NEW FORMS OF TRAINING

Apostolic networks and apostolic leaders in general are in agreement that traditional seminaries and Bible schools will continue to meet the needs of the churches that remain in the old wineskins indefinitely. But something different is needed for the Second Apostolic Age. What form will the new educational wineskin take? Apostolic leaders agree that there is no single form. A wide variety of training opportunities will be necessary to equip the saints of the churches that are part of the New Apostolic Reformation.

This became clear to me in 1998, when I convened an ad hoc meeting of 100 educators from a number of apostolic networks. The educators had all been moving from a paradigm of theological education, through which most of them had personally been schooled, to a new paradigm of equipping ministers. However, no two of them had developed the same design or were using the same methodologies. As the meeting progressed and the educators began to feel like kindred spirits, it became obvious that it would be impossible to agree on an ideal set of standards to which all could conform. For example, one network was assigned by God to train leaders of churches planted in university communities, while another to provide training to godly, gifted people who were illiterate.

NEW FORMS OF CHURCH WILL REQUIRE NEW FORMS OF LEADERSHIP TRAINING.

An immediate and somewhat iconoclastic implication of this, which would especially pop up in the minds of professional educators, was that traditional academic accreditation was irrelevant to them. To attempt to conform to known accreditation associations would be paramount to deciding to reenter the old wineskin. Rejection of accreditation, as I think back, turned out to be the strongest uniting force of the group. In spite of this, those present felt a need not to continue as lone rangers but rather to find some glue, other than accreditation, that would bind them together.

The concept that surfaced was to agree on a covenant of mutual accountability. Consequently, the Apostolic Council for Educational Accountability (ACEA) was formed. As of this writing, over 40 institutions have taken membership, paid dues and attended annual meetings. The schools that are members of ACEA exchange faculty, invite each other for on-site consultations and hold one another accountable, not for attaining a prescribed standard of teaching, but rather for implementing with integrity whatever assignment and calling God has given to each one. ACEA members, rather than seeing themselves as competitors, become cheerleaders for each other, anxious to affirm God's unique calling for fellow apostolically-oriented educators.

For those of us who have been involved in both the old wineskin of theological education and the new educational wineskin of equipping ministers, we recognize that the procedures have made a 180-degree turn. Here are some of the differences:

- **No academic requirements.** Accredited theological seminaries, because they require a college degree for entrance, have eliminated 75 percent of America's population from their student body. Apostolic institutions, on the other hand, want to be available to train all of God's saints for the work of the ministry.
- **Impartation along with information.** In the school that I lead, Wagner Leadership Institute (WLI), I instruct my faculty not to focus primarily on transferring a body of knowledge from their heads to the students' heads as much as imparting to them tools and anointing for fruitful ministry. As the students will tell you, they invariably suffer from information overload, but the information is secondary while the impartation is primary.
- **No exams or grades.** Because of the focus on impartation, I find it impractical to give exams or letter grades for the courses. The powerful impartation for ministry that the students receive validates the quality of their education, so exams and grades are not necessary.
- **No resident students or resident faculty.** Because we in WLI are training in-service, rather than preservice, ministers, it is impossible for most students to enter a residence program. The students have families, jobs, community involvements and ministries wherever they live. Most cannot give three years to full-time study. In addition, by using visiting faculty, it is possible to draw on the best in each field on a time-available basis.
- **Variable delivery systems.** The WLI delivery system does not

fit all ACEA institutions. Some institutions have residence programs, and some have required courses. Some offer weekly classes Thursday and Friday nights and Saturday mornings. Some have classes only one night per week. Some use retreats and conferences. Others will schedule occasional weeklong evening courses.

· **Curriculum.** Courses are tailor-made to the needs of the students. There are few required courses, on the supposition that those saints who are already experienced in ministry know better about what they need to be more effective than would a remote school administrator or an impersonal accrediting association. In any case, the old-wineskin ratio of 80 percent of curriculum being theory and (at best) 20 percent application is reversed. At least 80 percent of apostolic curriculum has a direct, practical application to active ministry. Saying this, however, must never soften the need for providing excellent biblical and theological foundations for every minister. The 20 percent is also very important.

A NEW APOSTOLIC DIRECTION

It is true that as we pursue these new forms of training, we can expect to receive our share of criticism from those of the traditional educational establishment. I have heard comments that our nonaccredited schools are diploma mills. Some argue that mutual accountability can never substitute for the integrity of academic accreditation. In fact, when I attempted to advertise WLI in a prominent evangelical Christian magazine, I was denied access because WLI wasn't accredited.

Nevertheless, the Second Apostolic Age is a reality, and changes are not coming sometime in the future—they are already here. The Spirit is speaking to the churches. In the field of leadership training, we are moving from theological education to equipping ministers.

CHAPTER NINE

FROM A HEAVY DOCTRINAL LOAD TO A LIGHTER DOCTRINAL LOAD

ALMOST 50 YEARS AGO, I NEARLY FLUNKED MY ORDI-
NATION EXAMINATION!

As I suggested in the last chapter, ordination examinations back in the mid 1950s were heavily weighted toward theology versus things like character, giftedness and practical skills for ministry. This was true of the members of my ordination committee. I must say that when I sat down for the examination, I was quite confident that I could pass, because I had just spent three years receiving graduate theological education in a prestigious seminary. However, I was in for a rather rude awakening. I had not become aware of how important certain theological nuances could become in the minds of some ministers.

THE TWO NATURES OF CHRIST

It so happened that one of my theological professors, Edward John Carnell, was popular with the students because from time to time he displayed a bit of theological creativity. Unlike many of his colleagues, he was not reluctant to occasionally color outside of standard theological lines. He happened to do this when I was taking the Christology segment of his systematic theology course. In it he taught us standard orthodox theology that Jesus had a fully divine nature as well as a fully human nature. Then Carnell postulated that on the basis of Philippians 2, we could well conclude that while Jesus was on Earth, He voluntarily gave up the use of (not the possession of) His divine attributes. Consequently, everything Jesus did on Earth, including His signs and wonders, He did through His human nature, empowered by the Holy Spirit.

This made good sense to me. Since I was a recent convert at the time, I had never been programmed with any conflicting ideas, so it was easy to accept Carnell's teaching. What I didn't fully realize was that probably 95 percent of evangelical theologians were teaching that Jesus, during His life on Earth, constantly switched back and forth between His divine and human natures. When He turned water into wine, for example, He would be using His divine nature; and when He got hungry, He would be functioning through His human nature.

The members of my ordination committee happened to be among the 95 percent. When they asked me about Jesus' natures, I naively gave Carnell's answer, not the answer they expected. When the examination was over and I was asked to leave the room, I soon began to suspect that they might have been taking a longer time than usual to call me back and give me their verdict. Sure enough, I later found out that there were some on the committee who thought that I should be denied ministerial ordination because of my view on the relationship between the natures of Christ. Fortunately, others were a bit more moderate, and I was told that my ordination would need to be postponed until I spent 20 hours in a seminary library reading up on Christology.

I dutifully put in my 20 hours in the seminary library. The upshot was that the more I read, the more I was convinced that my view was actually the most biblical one. I continue to hold that view by the way, and I have explained my position in writing. In fact, the fifth magazine article I ever published was on the subject, and later I wrote a whole chapter in a book on it.[1]

DOCTRINAL LOADS

My purpose in telling this story is not to suggest that my view on Christ's natures is necessarily the right one (even though I think it is). My only purpose here is to point out that such a relatively minor and debatable theological issue could have been, in the minds of some, a reason for disqualification for ordination to the Christian ministry. Members of my ordination committee seemed to me to be carrying a heavier-than-necessary doctrinal load.

As we in the Body of Christ have led up to and now entered the Second Apostolic Age, there has been a steady, although not particularly rapid, movement toward a lighter view of doctrine. By this I do not mean that apostolic leaders do not have strong convictions on biblical and theological issues. They do. Their biblical and theological convictions are as strong as they ever were. Nevertheless, there just don't seem to be as many doctrinal nuances as there used to be for which these leaders would choose to lay down their lives or, for that matter, for which they would refuse relationships with other brothers and sisters in Christ who may disagree.

Apostolic leaders are not theological illiterates. Nevertheless, they have little or no desire to traverse many of the traditional pathways laid down by professional academic theologians. A cursory glance at the titles of the articles in scholarly theological journals would be enough to keep most visionary, activist apostolic leaders at arm's length. Their evaluation of the theological articles wouldn't be based on whether they are right or wrong nearly as much as whether they are relevant to any conceivable aspect of practical ministry.

In the last chapter, I gave some reasons why I do not include any required courses in the Wagner Leadership Institute curriculum. For example, I have never offered a course in systematic theology simply because there would be virtually no demand for it among our in-service, apostolically oriented student body. This, I well know, would strike the traditional theological education establishment as unthinkable. How could we possibly award diplomas to students who had not subjected themselves to the discipline of scholarly theology? In old-wineskin schools, systematic theology is not optional; it is required for graduation.

THEOLOGY DEFINED

What is theology? This would be a good question to look at in order to put the whole thrust of this chapter in broad perspective. A dictionary would tell you that theology is "the study of God" because it is made up of two Greek roots: *theos*, meaning "God," and *logos*, meaning "science of" or "study of." But, moving beyond those basics, we also need to understand theology in a more functional dimension. In other words, what does it mean to *do* theology? I have seen long descriptions of all that contemporary theology involves, and I have concluded that, at least for me, most of them make doing theology much too complicated.

Here is what I think theology really amounts to: a human attempt to explain God's Word and God's works in a reasonable and systematic way.

Think about this for a moment. The phrase "human attempt" is a vital part of the definition because it separates theology from Scripture, which is not human but is divinely inspired. We do not argue with Scripture, but when it comes to our *explanations* of Scripture and *interpretations* of Scripture, the human dimension enters the picture to one degree or another, and we begin crossing over the line toward theology. Part of theology, I repeat, is our human attempt to explain God's Word.

THEOLOGY IS A HUMAN ATTEMPT TO EXPLAIN GOD'S WORD AND GOD'S WORKS IN A REASONABLE AND SYSTEMATIC WAY.

But that is not all. God did not stop revealing Himself and His will when the Bible was completed. He continues to be active in the world, and His works can be seen and understood. As we are told in the book of Revelation, the Holy Spirit continues to speak to the churches, and we must have an ear to hear (see Rev. 2:7). Doing theology, then, starts with understanding God's Word, but it goes on from there to understanding what God is saying and doing in the world today. This is the "God's works" part of the definition. Admittedly, the human dimension in this second part may be even more subjective than the human dimension in the first part, but both expose the same reality. Theology, per se, is not divinely inspired. It is a human activity.

LAYERS OF THEOLOGY

Let's imagine that theology is something like an onion. You can pull layer after layer off an onion until finally you get down to the core.

Theology also has many layers and a core. The further the layers of theology get from the core, the more the human dimension in doing theology comes into play.

The best explanation I have seen of these theological layers comes from Pastor Ted Haggard of New Life Church in Colorado Springs. With his permission, I have included his diagram that pictures the theological onion. The core is absolutes; the first layer is interpretations; the next is deductions; and the outer layers, where human perspectives can run wild, are subjective opinions, personal preferences, feelings, cultural norms and the like.

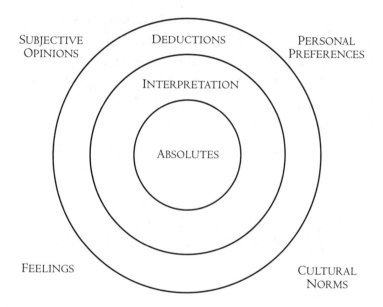

Absolutes

The inner circle of absolutes is extremely important, because it defuses the possibility that this view of theology might be devoid of passionate conviction. Ted Haggard calls them "the essentials of our faith" and "the foundation for everything else we believe."[2] God gives us some absolutes, several of which are His existence, the integrity of Scripture, the death and resurrection of Christ, and the existence of heaven and hell. There are other absolutes as well. But when Ted Haggard uses the word "we," he does not necessarily mean that all of the absolutes in New Life Church's inner circle apply to the entire Body of Christ. They likely have put into the absolutes circle some things that should be in the deductions circle, as does every church or denomination.

Broadening out from New Life Church, which is a typical apostolic church, to the apostolic movement in general, we will find that the total number of items included in the absolutes circles of apostolic leaders will generally be considerably smaller than it was in the old wineskin. Since there is no overarching apostolic agency that dictates what must be in everyone's absolutes circle, it would be expected that different churches and ministries and apostolic networks would end up with different sets of absolutes. However, all of the ministries that I know of would include three of the key theological premises of the Protestant Reformation: the authority of Scripture, justification by faith and the priesthood of all believers. Each one of these three signaled a significant departure from the theology of the old wineskin at the time of the Reformation: the Roman Catholic Church.

DO NOT CONCLUDE THAT ANY PERSONAL
INTERPRETATION OF SCRIPTURE
WHATSOEVER IS OKAY.

Interpretations

We can agree on the final authority of Scripture, but still it is necessary to draw meanings and applications from the words of Scripture. Some Scriptures, such as "Honor your father and your mother" (Exod. 20:12), are pretty clear as stated. Other Scriptures, such as "Sell whatever you have and give to the poor" (Mark 10:21), will undoubtedly need some interpretation. In most cases there can be more than one acceptable interpretation of a Bible passage, and those who interpret it differently should respect the other points of view.

Because the human dimension is strong here, we need to be on guard and recognize those who attempt to use human interpretations to *change* the meaning of the original Scripture. An example of this would be professing Christians who have chosen to become homosexual activists. Since many who attempt this profess to believe the Bible, they are then forced to come up with some alternative interpretation of those biblical passages that explicitly put homosexuality in the same category as adultery, stealing, murder and other sins. Most Christian leaders I know would not think that a great deal of interpretation is needed for a Scripture like Romans 1:26-27:

> God gave them up to vile passions. For even their women exchanged the natural use for what is against nature. Likewise also the men, leaving the natural use of the woman, burned in their lust for one another, men with men committing what is shameful, and receiving in themselves the penalty of their error which was due.

Attempting to force another meaning on this is unacceptable.

The reason I bring this up is to warn against concluding that any personal interpretation of Scripture whatsoever is okay. No. If the authority of Scripture is one of our absolutes, then twisting Scripture to justify ideas such as homosexuality as an alternate lifestyle for a believer will be firmly rejected.

Deductions

Ted Haggard contrasts interpretation and deduction:

> While an interpretation is explaining what a passage of Scripture means, deduction is taking one verse from one place in the Bible,

connecting it with a verse from another place, and then coming to a conclusion that would not be evident from either of the verses on its own.[3]

A large number of our theological positions are derived from deductions, as Haggard defines them. I agree with him when he says, "Most end-times theology is a deduction."[4] The popular Left Behind series of novels, for example, is premised on the *deduction* that toward the end of this age, all true believers will be raptured into heaven without dying, while those left on Earth will be subjected to seven years of grueling tribulation until Jesus finally returns to Earth and begins a glorious 1000-year reign. When I was in the old wineskin, this was part of my theological load. I was a member of the ranks of pretribulation-rapture premillennialists, and I was proud of it. I dared affirm my belief in what I considered a clear teaching of Scripture. If anyone would have suggested that I believed in what might have been a "deduction," I probably would have regarded that person as a deluded and uninformed liberal.

Do you see what I was doing? Although I didn't know it at the time, I was making the mistake of positioning a deduction in the absolutes circle. I later realized that by doing so, I was carrying a heavier doctrinal load than I needed to. Over the years, the more I matured and the more I began listening to deductions that others had reached from the same Scriptures, the more I began to admit that there must have been a good bit of human input to what I was then believing. I gradually eased my end-times theology out of the absolutes circle and into the deductions category. The net result is that end-times theology is a battle I no longer care to fight. If anyone asks me whether I am a premillennialist or an amillennialist or a postmillennialist, I really don't know. At that point I usually tuck my tongue into my cheek and say, "I'm a panmillennialist." When they give me a curious look, I say, "Sure. I believe everything's going to pan out all right!"

Not too many years ago, when we were carrying heavier doctrinal loads, a remark like that might well have cost me friends. Or it could have even prevented my ordination. But now we laugh at it. Why?

Because we are moving from a heavy doctrinal load to a lighter doctrinal load. Part of this translates into enjoying life more. Even though I do not support pretribulation-rapture theology, I have read every book in the Left Behind series and I have enjoyed every minute of what I regard as wholesome, fictional escape literature.

Ironically, because I locate end-times theology in the deduction circle, I must be honest enough to admit that there is a distinct possibility that I may be wrong and that Tim LaHaye and Jerry Jenkins, authors of the Left Behind novels, might be right in their view of the pretribulation rapture.

Although some denominations still regard end-times theology, such as premillenialism, as an absolute and make it a litmus test for ministerial ordination, most of my colleagues who are leaders in the Second Apostolic Age do not. They tend to hold whatever conclusion they might have adopted on eschatology, which is the theological term for end-times beliefs, lightly. They might not use Ted Haggard's terms, but conceptually they realize that we are dealing with deductions and not absolutes.

For the majority of us, admitting that our end-times theological positions are deductions—not absolutes—is relatively easy. However, it is a good deal harder to concede this on other theological issues. In the remainder of this chapter, I will present a few other issues in order of increasing difficulty or controversy. The next issue we will examine is Calvinism.

CLASSICAL CALVINISM

During the 40 years in which I ministered mostly within American denominational circles, the most prevalent theological mind-set that I encountered among church leaders was classical Calvinism or derivatives thereof. I am not saying that there were no respected leaders who held differing views—particularly the Arminianism common in denominations tracing their roots to John Wesley—because there were and still are. However, in seminary I was taught Reformed theology, i.e., Calvinism, as if it were *the* correct systematization of biblical truth. In other words, the tenets of Calvinism were actually theological deductions, but many Calvinistic theologians located them in the absolutes circle. People who disagreed would be considered either unintelligent or uninformed.

TULIP

Calvinism became popularly known by five points, which are spelled out by the acronym "TULIP." These points are

- Total depravity—Every human being since Adam is intrinsically sinful
- Unconditional election—God has chosen from the foundation of the world those whom He will save
- Limited atonement—Christ died only for those whom God elected for salvation
- Irresistible grace—Those whom God has elected will be saved no matter what
- Perseverance of the saints—Once saved, always saved

Fundamental to these five points is a view of the absolute sovereignty of God that causes us to postulate that even before God created human beings, He knew what every individual ever born would do and how they would end up both in this life and in the life to come. This is called foreknowledge. Since God had this perfect foreknowledge, it follows that before we were even born, questions like whether we would end up in heaven or in hell had already been determined in the mind of the Almighty. This is called predestination. If all this is true, it is easy to see where the TULIP ideas came from.

The Wilting TULIP

Part of the process of moving from a heavy doctrinal load to a lighter doctrinal load in the Second Apostolic Age is a notable wilting of the

TULIP, so to speak. This does not mean that Calvinism is dead. Many of the apostolic leaders of the new wineskin are strong Calvinists, but I think it is accurate to say that the TULIP has, for the most part, been moving from the absolutes circle of Ted Haggard's diagram into the deductions circle.

Limited atonement was one of the first doctrines of Calvinism to be deabsolutized by many. Most Bible believers tend to take literally statements like "For the love of Christ compels us, because we judge thus: that if One died for all, then all died, and He died for all" (2 Cor. 5:14-15). Unconditional election and irresistible grace seem to conflict with the human initiative implied in "Go into all the world and preach the gospel to every creature. He who believes and is baptized will be saved; but he who does not believe will be condemned" (Mark 16:15-16). Perseverance of the saints has hung in there quite strongly, but I have begun to hear sermons in recent years teaching that it must be possible for people who were once saved to lose their salvation. For a long time, I would have thought that was heresy, but now I see it as simply a reasonable theological deduction.

I discuss total depravity in more detail in the next chapter, where I explain that humans may be depraved but not so totally depraved that they cannot possibly live a truly holy life.

OPEN THEOLOGY

Over the past few years, a group of credible, respected theologians have proposed a way of understanding the nature of God that goes deeper than the five TULIP points, questioning the classical Calvinist view of God's foreknowledge. This is called open theology, or open theism, and it is espoused by such thinkers and authors as Greg Boyd, Clark Pinnock, John Sanders and others. Their arguments, in my opinion, might stop short of dealing a coup de grace to classical Calvinism, but at the very least they make it untenable to locate TULIP in or near the absolutes circle.

What does open theology teach? Based on a quantity of biblical evidence, it teaches that the sovereign God (God's sovereignty is not the issue) has so designed the world and His relationship to His creation that He has intentionally left many things up to decisions that human beings make, rather than predetermining them or foreknowing them. In other words, much of what human beings do really matters in determining history.

Does God Ever Change His Mind?

The key issue of open theology is reflected in the subtitle of Greg Boyd's excellent book, *God of the Possible: Does God Ever Change His Mind?* Boyd thinks that God does change His mind, and I happen to agree with him. I know that some will criticize me for espousing open theology, but in doing so I am not attempting to argue that it is a theological absolute and that others should agree with me. I am simply suggesting that open theology is a deduction based on biblical evidence concerning the nature of God, and that it is at least as reasonable as the deductions expressed in classical Calvinism or Arminianism for that matter.

Open theology is new to most, but I would expect that some who have always thought that God's foreknowledge of all things might be a theological absolute could conceive at least a hint of why I, along with others, think that open theology is a reasonable theological deduction. It seems clear, to take one example, that God actually changed His mind when Moses came down off the mountain and found the people worshiping a golden calf. God said, "I'm so angry with [these people] I am going to destroy them" (Exod. 32:10, *GOD'S WORD*). Moses replied, "Don't be so angry. Reconsider your decision to bring disaster to your people" (Exod. 32:12, *GOD'S WORD*). The upshot? "So the LORD reconsidered his threat to destroy his people" (Exod. 32:14, *GOD'S WORD*).

The Scriptures are peppered with similar incidents. My Calvinistic professors told me that we must interpret such passages as anthropomorphisms: expressions of the nature of God in terms that humans can understand but which should not be taken literally. However, to the contrary, open theology recommends that we take such passages literally—and why not?

Consider, for example, this Scripture in which God discusses His own nature:

> At one moment I may declare concerning a nation or a kingdom, that I will pluck up and break down and destroy it, but if that nation, concerning which I have spoken, turns from its evil, I will *change my mind* about the disaster that I intended to bring on it. And at another moment I may declare concerning a nation or a kingdom that I will build and plant it, but if it does evil in my sight, not listening to my voice, then I will *change my mind* about the good that I had intended to do to it (Jer. 18:7-10, *NRSV*, emphasis added).

Does God ever change His mind? If we take these Scriptures at face value, it is reasonable to think that, at least on occasion, He does. Consider Jonah's going to Nineveh. God said through Jonah: "In forty days Nineveh will be destroyed" (Jon. 3:4, *GOD'S WORD*). The king led his people in repentance. "God saw what they did. He saw that they turned from their wicked ways. So God reconsidered his threat to destroy them, and he didn't do it" (Jon. 3:10, *GOD'S WORD*).

Does Prayer Make a Difference?

What difference does having open theology make? In the years that I have spent in helping to lead the global prayer movement, I have found that most intercessors and prophets assume open theology. They may not use the term and they may not have read Greg Boyd's book, but they believe deep down that their prayers really have an effect on God's decisions in certain circumstances. For example, since it is clear that God is not willing that any should perish (see 2 Pet. 3:9), they pray for the salvation of the lost. Why? Because they believe that as a direct result of their prayers, some will be saved who otherwise would not. They would agree with Richard Foster, who says, "We are working with God to determine the future. Certain things will happen in history if we pray rightly."[5]

I love this quote from John Sanders:

Our prayers can have an effect on God's plans. It makes no sense
to say God grieves, changes his mind, and is influenced by our
prayers, and also claim that God tightly controls everything so
that everything that occurs is what God desired to happen![6]

Not everyone agrees that open theology should be regarded as simply another valid theological deduction. A case in point would be the
Evangelical Theological Society (ETS), made up of several hundred professional theologians from traditional evangelical denominations. Many
of them are not quite ready for the lighter doctrinal load accompanying
the Second Apostolic Age, particularly in the area of open theology. In
their November 2003 annual meeting, for example, a concerted effort
was made by a number of theologians to expel both Clark Pinnock and
John Sanders from ETS because of their open theology. In Sanders's
case, the vote to dismiss him failed by only a slight margin.[7]

INTERCESSORS PRAY FOR THE SALVATION OF THE
LOST BECAUSE THEY BELIEVE THAT AS A DIRECT
RESULT OF THEIR PRAYERS, SOME WILL BE SAVED
WHO OTHERWISE WOULD NOT.

THEOLOGY OF THE TRINITY

In this chapter's previous discussions of theological issues, from end-
times theology to classical Calvinism to Open theology, it was fairly
easy to see that various church traditions are human attempts to logically and systematically make deductions from Scripture. These
deductions clearly are a step or two removed from the absolutes, the

pure and direct revelation of God in Scripture.

Now we come to the theology of the Trinity. The Trinity certainly is a vital issue in Christian faith. In fact, millions of Christians through the ages have worshiped God as "Trinity." I am a convinced Trinitarian, and most of my friends and fellow leaders in the apostolic movement are Trinitarians, but not all of them. A few hold to the doctrine of Oneness.

I believe that all Christians experience the Trinity, but not all Christians necessarily describe that experience in the same way. I think the most sensible way to understand what the Bible says about the Father and the Son and the Holy Spirit is, to use the standard theological terminology, that they are three Persons in one essence. When I consider Jesus (the Son) being baptized in the Jordan, the voice of the Father speaking out from the heavenlies and the Holy Spirit descending on Him like a dove, I think, *How can you avoid the deduction that they are three persons, all of them being God?*

Historically, however, finding the best language to describe the Trinity has been one of the most complex of all theological issues. God's self-revelation through Christ and His teaching on the Holy Spirit raised very important questions. It took the Church's best minds, many consultations, synods and councils, and nearly 350 years to propose a suitable way of describing the Trinity. Finally, in A.D. 381 the Council of Constantinople established Trinitarianism as the understanding of all the State churches in the Roman Empire.

Oneness Theology

Oneness theologians also use the terms "Father," "Son" and "Holy Spirit," but they use them in a different way than Trinitarians do. Instead of three Persons, they see three different modes, or manifestations, of God, who is one Person. Back at the time of the Council of Nicea in A.D. 325, these theologians went not by the name of "Oneness," but by the name of "Modalism." The Council of Nicea rejected Modalism, and the great majority of Christian theologians through the centuries have assumed that Nicea was correct.

However, in 1914 a group of pastors from the early Pentecostal movement in the Assemblies of God resurrected the ancient Modalistic view of God. At first they called their movement "Jesus Only," and later the term "Oneness Pentecostalism" became the accepted designation. They were expelled in 1917 from the Assemblies of God, which regarded Trinitarianism as a theological absolute. In fact, of 585 ministers holding Assemblies of God credentials, no fewer than 156 were dismissed, along with their congregations.[8]

Some may be wondering why I am going into so much detail about the Oneness movement. While I do not consider Oneness theology a valid deduction, this movement did not stop when it was declared to be heretical in 1917. A large and, in fact, growing number of denominations have been spawned with a Oneness theology, denominations such as Pentecostal Assemblies of the World, Church of Our Lord Jesus Christ of the Apostolic Faith, United Pentecostal Church International (UPCI) and many others.[9] The United Pentecostal Church International is the largest Oneness denomination in the United States.

A Lighter Load

I am including this discussion on Oneness theology to raise this question: Should our view of the persons of God be a part of our absolutes theological category or a part of our deductions category? For example, all Christians are presented in the Bible with the many scriptural references to God as Father, to Jesus the Son and to the Holy Spirit. Trinitarian Christians in the West (Roman Catholics and Protestants) have fit these Scriptures together and used the term "Trinity" and the phrase "three Persons in one essence" to describe God's self-revelation. These theological terms and phrases are nowhere found in the Bible, but to Western Christians they suitably describe the biblical evidence. On the other hand, the Eastern Orthodox churches, appealing to the same biblical evidence, are also Trinitarians, yet they have chosen to avoid the language of "Persons." They prefer to say that the one true God has always existed as God the Father, God the Son and God the Holy Spirit.

In doing this the Eastern churches convey their theological deductions using language that is somewhat less restrictive.

Oneness Christians, for their part, have come to different conclusions from the same Scriptures.

WHILE THE MAJORITY OF APOSTOLIC LEADERS TODAY STILL HOLD STRONG PERSONAL CONVICTIONS ON THE TRINITY, WE ARE LIGHTENING OUR DOCTRINAL LOAD WHEN IT COMES TO CHOOSING WITH WHOM WE RELATE.

If I am not mistaken, most apostolic leaders today would agree that while Trinitarian theology might be a strong conviction to the majority of us, it might not be regarded as an absolute on which we would gauge our ability to support each other and work together in advancing God's kingdom. We seem to be somewhat more at ease with differences in our views of the Persons of the Godhead today than we might have been back in 1917, or perhaps in the earliest stages of the Church when some of these theological issues were still being debated and were in flux. While the majority of us still hold strong personal convictions on the Trinity, we are lightening our doctrinal load when it comes to choosing with whom we relate.

TENURE EXAMINATION

I began by describing how I almost flunked my ordination examination. Let me now add the story of how I actually did flunk my first examination for academic tenure at Fuller Theology Seminary. Although I didn't know it at the time, I now see that this also illustrates a methodology employed by the corporate spirit of religion in attempting to block this new move of God in the area of our attitude toward doctrinal loads.

After I had taught in seminary for a time, my career reached the point when I would be considered for faculty tenure. Part of the process was to be examined theologically by professional theologians from the School of Theology, even though my specialty was missiology in the School of World Missions. During the examination, one theologian asked, "What do you think of systematic theology?" I replied, "Well, as a starter I do not think that we should refer to 'systematic theology' in the singular as if there were only one valid systematic theology. The Bible is absolute, but theologies are merely human attempts to systematize the way we interpret what the Bible teaches. Particularly in cross-cultural situations, different systematic *theologies* (plural) would be expected to emerge in different cultures."

This was like setting off a firecracker in a funeral parlor! It was not the answer that the theologians expected. As they cross-examined me, they asked for examples of how theology could possibly vary from culture to culture. In their minds, theology was close to absolute. That, as I see it now, was a mind-set produced and nurtured by the corporate spirit of religion.

So I brought up the doctrine of the Trinity. I reiterated that I considered myself a solid Trinitarian, but then I said, "My passion is to see multitudes of unsaved people come to Jesus Christ. Some of the most resistant peoples of the whole world are Muslims and Jews. It is a recognized fact that top-level, conscientious, educated, good-hearted Muslim and Jewish leaders sincerely believe that we Christians are tritheists. They claim that they believe in only one God, but that Christians believe in three Gods: Father, Son and Holy Spirit. We know that we are just as monotheistic as Muslims and Jews, but they can't see it. It would really be nice if our professional systematic theologians could somehow reword our doctrine of the Trinity, and thus speed up the fulfillment of the Great Commission."

Not surprisingly, I flunked my tenure examination!

Let me add, as a footnote, that grace ultimately prevailed. The theologians generously invited me back for a second chance. This second time I wisely did not bring up the doctrine of the Trinity, and they awarded me tenure.

A LIGHT STATEMENT OF FAITH

Most of the statements of faith that I have signed and subscribed to during my career are classical Trinitarian statements of faith. I had no problem because I fit. In fact, most were what I now call heavy: packing large numbers of theological issues into what would be regarded as the absolutes category. For example, back in 1974 I signed the Lausanne Covenant, a statement containing 30,000 words.

I was never faced with writing a new statement of faith until I founded Wagner Leadership Institute in 1998. By then, I was aware that the New Apostolic Reformation was characterized by moving from a heavier doctrinal load to a lighter one. I also knew that I didn't want to exclude Oneness Christians.

The statement of faith that I came up with was light—only 122 words long. It contains absolutes such as the Apostles' Creed, authority of Scripture, justification by faith, the priesthood of all believers, Jesus' virgin birth, His resurrection, heaven and hell, and the like. On the Godhead, it simply says that we believe that God is Father, Son and Holy Spirit. Both Trinitarians and Oneness Pentecostals can sign off on that as an absolute. If we go from there to the issue of persons, we enter the realm of deductions.

A NEW APOSTOLIC DIRECTION

A whole new generation of believers in the Second Apostolic Age is not nearly as interested in the fine points and details of theology as past generations have been. Few people choose their church these days because of what it believes about open theology or Calvinism or modes of baptism or church government or the pretribulation rapture or sanctification or predestination or the forensic theory of justification. If God is our Father and if we are saved through Jesus' blood shed on the cross and if we are daily filled with and empowered by the Holy Spirit, I am convinced we can find a way to work together despite our theological differences.

Let's not overcrowd our inner circle of theological absolutes. If we do, the exciting new streams flowing from what the Spirit is saying to the churches may pass us by.

CHAPTER TEN

FROM REFORMED SANCTIFICATION TO WESLEYAN HOLINESS

I WOULD GUESS THAT OVER THE PAST FIVE YEARS OR SO, I HAVE HEARD MORE MESSAGES AND READ MORE ARTICLES AND BOOKS ON HOLINESS THAN IN THE PREVIOUS 35 YEARS COMBINED.

What has brought about this change?

APOSTOLIC AUTHORITY AND CHARACTER

I believe the new emphasis on holiness is directly related to the transition that the Church is making into the Second Apostolic Age. As I have mentioned numerous times, the characteristic that most clearly distinguishes apostles from other members of the Body of Christ is the extraordinary authority that God delegates to them as individuals.

The measure of authority that God delegates to an apostle is much greater than the authority that leaders of the old wineskins of traditional Christianity ever had. The final authority in the old wineskins was almost invariably located in groups, with the idea that whatever authority the group had was shared among its members, although not always equally. Individual authority, consequently, was regarded as only a part of the whole. True, some strong leaders in the old wineskins succeeded in exercising a good deal of authority, but it was always subject to a number of checks and balances built into the organization.

A significant part of the criticism mustered by traditional leaders who are uncomfortable with the office of apostle is verbalized around the issue of authority. Apostles are frequently stereotyped as "dictators," "authoritarian," "on ego trips," "tyrants," "autocratic" or "empire builders." Somehow, in the minds of those embedded in the old wineskin, exercising strong authority is supposedly related to inevitable character flaws. The train of thought must run something like this: All apostles are dictators; all dictators are reprehensible; therefore all apostles are reprehensible. I have also heard the following common axiom used with the intent of nailing down the antiapostle argument: Power corrupts and absolute power corrupts absolutely. This mind-set sounds very much like another obvious tactic of the corporate spirit of religion:

to work on people's minds to preserve the religious status quo.

As I have observed apostles over the past few years—most of whom have been personally confronted with charges like this more than once—I have found that their responses tend to follow a pattern. First, most of them try not to be defensive. They are acutely aware that the authority they have been given constantly runs the risk of crossing the line into ungodly dictatorship. Second, the criticisms, rather than offend apostles, more frequently put the fear of God into them. They fully agree that they must be on constant guard against abusing their power.

In fact, I know many Christian leaders who unmistakably are gifted apostles but who have hesitated to accept the *office* of apostle. A frequent reason for that is their awareness of the biblical principle that to whom much is given, much is required. With the public recognition of the office comes an expectation on the part of the general public for higher levels of accountability, vulnerability and holiness on the part of apostles. Some gifted leaders intuitively prefer to avoid this potential discomfort, and they remain at lower levels.

A STRICTER STANDARD OF JUDGMENT

This chapter is on the subject of holiness. I know it will seem strange to some that I just suggested that certain members of the Body of Christ, such as apostles, are expected to meet higher standards of holiness than others. The usual supposition is that God's standards of holiness are the same for everyone, but let's look at this a bit more closely. I think it might be correct to assume that God's standards are the same for all. I think it is equally correct that as far as His *judgment* is concerned, He cuts more slack for some than for others, and for apostles He cuts very little slack.

Let me explain by going to the rather familiar Scripture James 3:1: "My brethren, let not many of you become teachers, knowing that we shall receive a stricter judgment." The obvious meaning of this is that God has a double standard of judgment. He will judge teachers, of which James considers himself one, with a stricter judgment than He will judge those who are not teachers.

How does this apply to apostles?

In Ephesians 4:11, teachers are only one in a list of five church leadership offices that also includes pastors, evangelists, prophets and apostles. Logically, all individuals who fit this list would be subject to stricter levels of judgment. And when we carry this thought further and go to 1 Corinthians 12:28, we find that "God has appointed these in the church: first apostles, second prophets, third teachers." In the original Greek, these numbers, "first," "second" and "third," do not mean a random list, but rather a divine ordering. If this is true, we can conclude that God will undoubtedly judge apostles even more strictly than teachers. No wonder, then, that some people are nervous about being recognized as apostles.

GOD WILL UNDOUBTEDLY JUDGE APOSTLES EVEN MORE STRICTLY THAN TEACHERS. NO WONDER, THEN, THAT SOME PEOPLE ARE NERVOUS ABOUT BEING RECOGNIZED AS APOSTLES.

Related to this are the biblical passages that list requirements for church leadership roles such as bishops, presbyters, elders, deacons and the like. One of the classics is 1 Timothy 3, which begins, "A bishop then must be blameless" (v. 2). A detailed list of other character traits follows. This Scripture is obviously drawing a line between certain character traits required of a bishop that are not, at least to one degree or another, equally required of believers who are not bishops. If these qualifications apply to bishops, even more would they apply to apostles.

HUMBLY HOLY APOSTLES

What I have just said is not news to most of the apostles I know. They are extremely responsible individuals. They know the standards.

They have the fear of God in them, and they live their lives with a deter-mination to meet His standards of holiness. Most of them, as a matter of fact, do meet God's standards. Most apostles, in a word, are holy. The statement "Most apostles are holy" will require a good bit of elaboration. Its implications are tremendous, not only for apostles, but also for those whom they lead.

Before I begin to explain this statement, however, let me make an important assertion up front: While most apostles know that they are holy, and as a matter of fact they shudder to think of what might happen to them and their ministries if they weren't, the thought *I am holier than thou* never enters their mind. Their point of departure is not comparing their character with that of other believers but of comparing their character with God's standards.

An indispensable facet of apostolic character is humility. Biblically, it would be incongruous to imagine a true apostle who is not humble. Follow the logic: Jesus said, "He who humbles himself will be exalted" (Matt. 23:12). God has exalted apostles—they are first in order according to 1 Corinthians 12:28. If what Jesus said is true, God would not allow individuals to have the gift and office of apostle if they had not demon-strated their obedience to Jesus and humbled themselves. My point here is that apostolic humility defuses any inclination to imagine *I am holier than thou.*

THE REFORMED DOCTRINE OF SANCTIFICATION

Now let's get to the title of this chapter: "From Reformed Sanctification to Wesleyan Holiness."

The Protestant Reformation, under its two best-known leaders, Martin Luther and John Calvin, provided us a theological infrastructure that has carried us nobly for 500 years and undoubtedly will continue to carry us well into the future. In the last chapter I mentioned that the Reformed principles such as the authority of Scripture, justification by faith and the priesthood of all believers belong in the absolutes inner core of apostolic doctrine. I want to make it clear that nothing I say in this chapter is in the least bit intended to question the Reformers' unmatched role as history-changing Christian theologians who gave us a set of doctrinal absolutes that we will not compromise.

However, Luther and Calvin would be among the first to assure anyone who would ask that they were far from perfect. By implication, then, because they were not perfect, it follows that some of their theological conclusions might be questionable and consequently not really warrant a place in our absolutes circle of doctrine today. In the last chapter, for example, I mentioned some conclusions related to TULIP that I feel should be located in our deductions circle, not in the absolutes circle.

There is at least one more. I am now convinced that Luther's and Calvin's view of holiness, commonly known by the technical term "Reformed doctrine of sanctification," was one of their areas of weakness. I believe that God, in His providence, raised up John Wesley around 200 years later to bring the necessary corrections to the Body of Christ. His view is known by the term "Wesleyan holiness."

Total Depravity

As I have mentioned previously, the seminaries in which I was trained, Fuller and Princeton, both explicitly identified themselves as Reformed seminaries. That means that they generally accepted the views of Luther and Calvin—especially Calvin—as their theological bedrock. Consequently, it is no surprise that they taught that the Reformed doctrine of sanctification was *the* most biblical and *the* most correct view of holiness.

One of the core doctrines of Calvinism, the *T* in TULIP, is the total depravity of humans. This means that, as a consequence of Adam's disobedience in the Garden of Eden, human nature became permanently sinful. Individuals, of course, can be saved by God's grace, and their sins can be forgiven; nevertheless, their sinful human nature will persist until they die. They can be confident that, if they believe in Jesus Christ as their Savior, they will assuredly go to heaven when they die. But their life here on Earth will never be free from sin. As believers mature, they should grow in holiness and become more Christlike, but genuine personal holiness, or freedom from sin, will always remain beyond reach.

Compulsory Confession

The Calvinistic tenet of total depravity is why confession of sin has gained such a prominent, some would say exaggerated, place in the lives of Lutherans, Presbyterians, Reformed and the like. For example, some faithful Reformed believers not only confess sins every Sunday when they go to church, but they also confess sins when they pray in the morning, when they pray in the evening and when they say grace at each meal. Some of them will respond, "What's wrong with that? You can never confess enough!" Let's think about it a bit. Let's cut down to some of the assumptions behind such compulsory confession.

Suppose I confess my sins at breakfast. If I do, I expect that God will forgive any sins I have committed up to that point in time. But suppose that by force of habit, I know at breakfast that a few hours later I will also confess my sins at lunch. What am I presupposing? I'm presupposing that I will sin again that morning. At lunch I will assume that sometime after breakfast I sinned and that I once again need to confess. If someone were to ask what particular sin I had committed between meals, I might not be able to name it specifically; but my response might well be that, although I might not have been involved in a sin of commission, I could not possibly have avoided some sins of omission.

The notion that I actually could be holy and go, let's say, a whole day without sinning and at night have nothing specific to confess would display an arrogant attitude in the minds of those permeated with the Reformed doctrine of sanctification. Many of them would say that such an attitude, in itself, should be confessed as a sin!

Dr. Good's Essay

Let me give a concrete example of the implications of holding a Reformed doctrine of sanctification. I have before me an actual recent magazine article written by one of America's most respected evangelical theologians, who teaches future Christian workers at an extremely prestigious seminary. I know him personally, and I highly respect his character and his integrity, to say nothing of his scholarly brilliance. Other than disclosing his gender, I am going to mask his identity. I am not criticizing him personally. I am simply citing him as a distinguished representative of the Reformed doctrine of sanctification. Let's call him Dr. Good.

Dr. Good wrote an essay analyzing the phrase "The Lord make His face shine upon you." His key thought is that he does not see God's face shining on him, and because he is "an inveterate sinner," he does not know why it would.

This theologian's spiritual self-image is obviously very low. His term "inveterate" means "confirmed in a habit, practice or feeling"; "firmly established by long continuance"; "chronic."[1] He, therefore, would see himself as a hopelessly chronic sinner, unable to avoid the practice of sin on a daily basis. Little wonder that those who agree with him would feel that they could never confess enough.

Dr. Good would undoubtedly take issue with me when I make the statement that most apostles I know are, in fact, holy. The Reformed doctrine of sanctification would contend that even saying such a thing is another indicator that apostles tend to suffer from sinful delusions of grandeur.

WESLEYAN HOLINESS

John Wesley was one of the first to exhibit his dissatisfaction with the Reformed doctrine of sanctification. His study of the Bible convinced him, not only that believers could attain personal holiness, but also that God expected them to do that very thing. Personally, it took me quite a while to admit that there was any validity in Wesley's view, which is reflected today by Methodists, Nazarenes, Wesleyans, Church of God (Anderson, Indiana), Pentecostal Holiness, Salvation Army and many other denominations. A major reason was that my seminary professors had taught me, not only the Reformed doctrine of sanctification, but also how to soundly refute what they considered the flawed ideas underlying Wesleyan holiness.

JOHN WESLEY'S STUDY OF THE BIBLE CONVINCED HIM, NOT ONLY THAT BELIEVERS COULD ATTAIN PERSONAL HOLINESS, BUT ALSO THAT GOD EXPECTED THEM TO DO THAT VERY THING.

I turned the corner in the early 1990s when I became active in helping to move the Body of Christ into a mode of aggressive, strategic-level spiritual warfare. One of my first mentors in this paradigm shift was Cindy Jacobs of Generals of Intercession. I will not soon forget one of her early admonitions. She said that when we go into warfare, we need to put on the full armor of God. (The idea of putting on the armor was common knowledge at that time.) But then she went on to add words to this effect: "Even after we put on the full armor of God, if we do not have under that armor a pure heart, we will have holes in our armor!" This was enough to put the fear of God into me.

To be honest, until that time, I had not been overly concerned with having a pure heart because my Reformed doctrine of sanctification had informed me that I could never have one in this life. So, taking what Cindy had said at face value, I had two choices: (1) Keep away from spiritual warfare because, without a pure heart, I would have holes in my armor and therefore be vulnerable to the fiery darts of Satan; or (2) change my view of sanctification to Wesleyan holiness, which could point me in the direction of attaining a pure heart. Since my involvement in spiritual warfare was an assignment directly from God, I knew that I needed to make the second choice and to explore the biblical and theological validity of the kind of sanctification that could end up with a pure heart.

OUR REQUIREMENT

In order to do that, I didn't join a Methodist or a Wesleyan or a Nazarene Church. I just went back to the Scriptures to study about having a pure heart. When I did, I quickly found that the holiness about which John Wesley had attempted to communicate to the Body of Christ was not optional—it was absolutely essential—for those of us who were trying to move aggressively into spiritual warfare.

Let me explain something of what I found.

To begin with a key biblical quote, let's look at 1 Peter 1:15: "As He who called you is holy, you also be holy in all your conduct." All Christians generally agree that holiness is very important. However, I have noticed that many Christian leaders, especially those who hold the Reformed doctrine of sanctification, tend to slant their teaching about holiness toward the holiness of God. Since the holiness of God indisputedly belongs in the absolutes circle of doctrine of all believers, camping there is safe ground. In many ways, dealing with God's holiness is easier than dealing without personal holiness.

For example, if you ask a church music director to sing a song about holiness, in a large number of cases the director will predictably select the classic "Holy, Holy, Holy! Lord God Almighty." However, when you analyze the lyrics, you'll see that the song focuses on God's indisputable holiness, not on our personal holiness. It contains a line that reflects the Reformed doctrine of sanctification: "Only Thou art holy." Suppose we take that literally. If we do, it means that since God is the *only* being who truly is holy, you and I could never be holy unless we became God, which of course is absurd. Holiness, therefore, is out of our reach.

On the contrary, it is imperative that we take both parts of 1 Peter 1:15 at face value. Reformed theologians tend to highlight the first part, "As He who called you is holy," affirming God's holiness; but they tend to downplay the second part, "You also be holy in all your conduct."

Most apostles would conclude that God would never ask us to do something that was impossible. So if God asks us to be holy, as He does in 1 Peter 1:15, not only can we be holy, but also being holy basically boils down to our obedience.

Let's take some time to think this through.

OUR CHOICE TO OBEY

The book of James has a good bit to say about holiness. One of the strongest passages begins in the middle of chapter 3 and ends with verses 7 and 8 of chapter 4. Those two verses have four active verbs that help point the way toward holiness:

- Submit to God
- Draw near to God
- Cleanse your hands
- Purify your hearts

The first two of these actions that the Bible tells us to take—submitting to God and drawing near to Him—have to do with relationship with God. The second two—cleansing our hands and purifying our hearts—have to do with our behavior, or "conduct" (1 Pet. 1:15).

How do we go about this? Obviously our relationship with God is the starting point, but by itself it is not enough. Our attitude is important, but attitude will not make us holy. The presence of God is necessary, but God's presence is not the key variable. Take, for example, Adam and Eve. There was a time when they were holy and a time when they were no longer holy, and God was present with them during both times.

What, then, was the key factor with Adam and Eve? It was either adhering or not adhering to God's standards. They chose to disobey. Holiness, then, is not so much dependent on God's presence in our lives as it is on our choice to obey God.

Faith is an essential starting point, but keep in mind that faith can be dead. What brings faith to life? Our behavior! The Bible teaches that faith without works is dead (see Jas. 2:17-18). No one else can do our works for us. The choice is ours.

I know that this is strong teaching. Martin Luther, for one, couldn't stand it. He was reacting so much against the Roman Catholic teaching that salvation comes through works—not from faith alone—that he wished the book of James wasn't in the Bible. At one point he reportedly referred to it as an epistle of straw!

COUNTERCULTURAL HOLINESS

For 13 years, I taught a Sunday School class called the 120 Fellowship. It was a well-knit, loving group of around 100 adults. The members cared deeply for one another—that is, until I taught about holiness for three months. Before the three months were over, we had lost five families from the class, two of them the most influential families we had. The idea that holiness emerged from our decision to live according to God's standards was too much for them. Relationships trumped conduct in their minds. They wanted mercy, but not judgment.

The families who left our Sunday School class were flowing with the American culture of the time. They saw biblical holiness as countercultural. Researcher George Barna contrasts biblical holiness with American Christian culture:

> The Bible clearly states that true believers should be readily distinguished from nonbelievers by the way they live. Yet, the evidence undeniably suggests that most American Christians today do not live in a way that is quantifiably different from their non-Christian peers, in spite of the fact that they profess to believe in a set of principles that should clearly set them apart.[2]

HAGIOS

Barna's final words, "set them apart," go to the heart of biblical holiness. The Greek word for holy is *hagios*, meaning to be set apart. Hagios has two dimensions, namely being set apart *to* and being set apart *from*. Interestingly, every major biblical passage on holiness contains a list of explicit standards. They tell us what we must be set apart *to* and also what we must be set apart *from*. Take, for example, Colossians 3. In verse 12 the apostle Paul addresses "the elect of God, holy and beloved." Within the previous 11 verses, Paul lists 12 areas of conduct that, if we are holy, we are to be set apart *from* (fornication, evil desire, idolatry, filthy language, etc.); and in the following verses, he lists 12 areas of conduct that, if we are holy, we are to be set apart *to* (meekness, forgiveness, love, the husband's love for his wife, the wife's submission to her husband, etc.). God's standards are not vague; they are quite specific.

LEGALISM

The New Testament's expectation of holiness is not legalistic; it is relational. Since we love God, we naturally want to please Him. All the Bible is doing is telling us what pleases God and what doesn't please Him. These lists are very valuable if we want to maintain our personal relationship with Him on the highest level. Nothing could be clearer than 1 John 2:3 in that regard: "Now by this we know that we know Him [relationship], if we keep His commandments [obedience]." It goes on, "He who says, 'I know Him,' and does not keep His commandments, is a liar, and the truth is not in him" (v. 4).

The reason that I bring up legalism is that unfortunately some who were following the stream of Wesleyan holiness allowed themselves to fall into the trap of establishing the kind of carnal regulations for the behavior of their church members that Paul warned against: "'Do not touch, do not taste, do not handle,' which all concern things which perish with the using—according to the commandments and doctrines of men" (Col. 2:21-22). These religiously legal requirements had little to do with adhering to the standards of God. Fortunately, this legalism is not as prevalent today as it was two or three generations ago. However, some who were personally wounded by legalism for one reason or another turned not only against legalism but unfortunately also against holiness in general.

OUR POWER TO BE HOLY

If being holy or not being holy depends, in the final analysis, on our personal choices, where do we get the power to make the right choices? We don't have the power within us, because we have a sinful nature. This power only comes from being filled with the Holy Spirit. That is why it is important that we ask God to fill us with the Holy Spirit at the beginning of each day. He promises to do it if we simply ask (see Luke 11:9-13). Part of the package of being filled with the Holy Spirit is that He will convict us of sin, righteousness and judgment (see John 16:8). That means that when we step out of bounds and do something that does not please God, we will know it for sure because the Holy Spirit within us will let us know.

THE POWER TO MAKE RIGHT CHOICES ONLY COMES FROM BEING FILLED WITH THE HOLY SPIRIT.

I am saying all this to help give us confidence that we actually can be holy. Let me get personal about this: I happen to be writing this paragraph in the afternoon. So far today I have not sinned. I say "so far" because I don't think I will ever be in the place where sin could not enter my life before the day is over. I believe that some holiness denominations have gone to an extreme with doctrines of eradication and sinless perfection. They teach that when we receive the second blessing of the Holy Spirit, namely sanctification, we no longer need to be concerned about committing any more sins. I have serious doubts about that.

Even though I don't agree with eradication, I am still planning to live the rest of today without sinning. What do I base this expectation on? Every morning I pray the Lord's Prayer, which is given in Matthew 6:9-13. My habit is that when I pray, "Forgive my sins as I forgive those who sin against me," I do a mental review of the past 24 hours to see if I have any sin that needs to be confessed. This morning when I prayed, I had nothing to confess. How could I be sure? I am filled with the Holy Spirit, and He brought nothing to my mind.

That doesn't mean that He never convicts me of sin. But when He does, I know exactly what to do about it. I confess my sin, and He is faithful and just to forgive my sin and to cleanse me from all unrighteousness (see 1 John 1:9). That wipes my slate clean. My sin is now as far from me as the east is from the west. I'm ready to move into a new day, and I don't have to confess it again.

No sin yesterday? How about today? This morning I also prayed, "Lead me not into temptation," and I expect the Lord to answer that prayer all day long. If I am not tempted, I will not sin. Then, just to make sure, I asked the Lord to deliver me from the evil one. If Satan, the one who does the tempting, can't touch me, I definitely will not be tempted to sin.

My conclusion is that if I can go one day without sinning, I can go another day, and I can go for any number of days. But I keep praying and staying filled with the Holy Spirit, because I know that at any time—often when least expected—sin can invade my life. When (I did not say "if") it happens, I will have to deal with it immediately.

APOSTOLIC HOLINESS

Now, let's return to apostles and their holiness.

A while ago I mentioned that the biblical demands for holiness are stricter for leaders in general and apostles in particular. All of the character requirements listed in 1 Timothy 3 are high standards, but none is higher than the first: that an apostle must be blameless.

If we look at the apostle Paul as a role model of a biblical apostle, we can learn a good bit about how personal holiness is applied in real life. First Corinthians is a rather scathing letter that Paul wrote to the believers in Corinth, taking them to task for blatant misbehavior such as causing divisions, accusing each other in secular court, eating meat offered to idols, getting drunk at the Lord's Supper, rebelling, promoting heresy regarding the resurrection, living immorally, abusing the gift of tongues and more. Paul is undoubtedly anticipating that some who read the letter will say, "Who does this so-called apostle think he is? If the truth is known, he's probably as bad as we are."

With that possibility in mind, Paul very clearly says to the Corinthians, "For I know nothing against myself" (1 Cor. 4:4). This means that Paul has examined himself to see if there is anything pending that he should confess, and at the moment he finds nothing. He finds himself blameless. In other words, he is holy. He quickly adds that he is not saved or justified by his blameless conduct, but because of it he does feel qualified to call the Corinthians on the carpet.

Look at it this way. Paul exercises apostolic authority because he is blameless, as he is supposed to be in his leadership position. This is not pride, or a lack of humility. It is simply displaying his character credentials, without which he would not be able to function fully as an apostle. Admitting that there might be an exception here and there, I assert that the apostles I am related to today can say the same words that Paul wrote about himself to the Corinthians. That is why I have made the statement that most apostles are holy.

Once Paul affirmed that he personally was blameless, the door was open for him to say, "Therefore I urge you, imitate me" (1 Cor. 4:16). This is what apostles say, whether explicitly or implicitly, to their followers: "Examine what I do—how I conduct my life and how I make decisions and how I treat my spouse and other people and how I handle my finances and how I pray and whatever else I do—and you do the same if you want to please the Lord." These are strong words, but they have a biblical apostolic precedent.

Nothing here implies that Paul or any apostle today is perfect. But what it does imply is that apostles live lives that meet God's standards. They are in compliance with 1 Peter 1:15: "As He who called you is holy, you also be holy in all your conduct."

A New Apostolic Direction

The understanding of biblical data that most clearly opens the door for this apostolic lifestyle is Wesleyan holiness, not Reformed sanctification. This is the direction that the apostolic movement is taking these days.

CHAPTER ELEVEN

HISTORY MAKERS

THERE ARE A NUMBER OF DIFFERENT WAYS THAT PEOPLE REGARD HISTORY:

- Some ignore history.
- Some read and study history for the enjoyment of knowing more about the past.
- Some analyze history with the goal of deriving lessons from the past that can be applied to the future.
- Some love history and try to relive it.
- Others *make* history.

I want to be a history maker, and I know that there are many others out there who agree. If you are a believer, there has never been a better time for you to make history. In the Second Apostolic Age, we are already living through the most radical change in our way of doing church since the Protestant Reformation.

In each chapter of this book, I have highlighted and analyzed a number of these changes in some detail. In conclusion, I want to summarize what has been said and to restate some of the major thoughts in a simple and concise way.

NEW WINESKINS

A biblical analogy that I have used throughout to help us to understand our history-making task more clearly is Jesus' picture of old and new wineskins.

Old wineskins are strongly appealing. They offer a great deal of comfort and security. Jesus said, "No one, having drunk old wine, immediately desires new; for he says 'The old is better'" (Luke 5:39). Therefore, the majority of people will never desire to move into the new wineskins of the Second Apostolic Age. Consequently, they will never join the ranks of history makers. Why do they resist? Moving from an old wineskin to a new wineskin seems to be too much of a risk!

History makers, on the other hand, have always been risk takers.

Those who hear what the Spirit is now saying to the churches get excited about change. World changers will not tolerate the status quo.

THERE HAS NEVER BEEN A BETTER TIME TO MAKE HISTORY!

THE CORPORATE SPIRIT OF RELIGION

A major train of thought running through this book relates to the activity of the corporate spirit of religion. In order to refresh our memories, here is my definition of the spirit of religion: The spirit of religion is an agent of Satan assigned to prevent change and to maintain the status quo by using religious devices.

In most of this book's chapters, I pointed out how the corporate spirit of religion attempts to keep leaders from moving into God's new wineskins. In this concluding chapter, let me summarize what I have said.

The last thing that the spirit of religion wants you to be is a world changer. It would like you to be so comfortable with the past that, for the rest of your life, you would prefer to keep doing the things you have been doing.

How does the spirit of religion attempt to maintain the status quo in the Church today?

- The spirit of religion would love to maintain the status quo of denominational leadership, which prevents apostles from ministering in their God-given apostolic authority. It does this by casting a spell that convinces denominational leaders that final decisions affecting what the Church does must always be made by groups, not by individuals. In many cases, it has succeeded in elevating the notion of democratic church government to a level usually reserved only for essential doctrines.

- Thirty years of attempting to pour the new wine of the power of the Holy Spirit and of theological orthodoxy into decaying old wineskins of denominational structures has now been seen as a well-intentioned but fruitless effort. The spirit of religion would like reform-minded leaders to do the same for another 30 years, rather than take the bold step of moving and establishing separate apostolic networks.

- A growing number of believers are beginning to realize that what they are doing in the workplace six days a week can be considered as legitimate a Christian ministry assignment from God as what they do in their local congregations. The spirit of religion sees this as a threatening development to its evil purposes. It therefore tries to block the idea that the people of God in the workplace constitute a legitimate segment of the true Church and that this extended Church is founded on apostles and prophets just as the nuclear Church is.

- In the past, family heritage has been one of the strongest factors in determining a believer's church affiliation. Today, many church leaders are perceiving that affiliating with churches of other denominations in a given city can produce more effective ministry than restricting their contacts to those with their same heritage. The spirit of religion tries to discredit this change by convincing denominational power brokers that they should preserve the traditions of the elders at all costs.

- Church leaders in the Second Apostolic Age are now looking beyond enlarging their congregations, although this remains important, to penetrating all levels of society with the values and principles of the kingdom of God. The spirit of religion attempts to keep this vision bottled up because it knows that if it is applied, Satan will end up with much less control of society and finances than he has now.

- The spirit of religion is strongly attempting to create a Christian antiwar movement, persuading believers that if they do spiritual warfare and attempt to confront the devil and his principalities and powers, they have a good chance of becoming casualties. Christian pacifists make the spirit of religion happy.

- Despite the fact that research shows that traditional theological education does not necessarily produce competent church leaders, the spirit of religion persists in trying to make seminary and Bible school training a prerequisite for ministerial ordination.

- The unity of the Body of Christ is very important for the fulfillment of God's purposes on Earth. It is no secret that differences in doctrine have contributed to a great deal of division. Doctrine, however, is becoming less divisive in the Second Apostolic Age, and the spirit of religion is trying to thwart this trend.

- The devil can make more progress against a Church populated with less-than-holy believers than he can against a Church of holy believers. It would be to the advantage of the spirit of religion to preserve the mind-set that in this life we can never be holy.

RENEWAL OF THE MIND

The remedy for being under the spell of the spirit of religion in every one of the above scenarios is a new way of thinking. In chapter 1, I explained that the Hebrew word "belaw" characterizes the tactics of the corporate spirit of religion. This word means to wear out the victim in a *mental* sense. How do we defeat the enemy in this arena? We become transformed by the renewing of our *minds* as we are told to do in Romans 12:2. To move ahead, then, we need a paradigm shift.

My purpose in this book is to help us change our minds so that we can be history makers, not mere maintainers of the status quo. God has given us the power to overthrow the spirit of religion. Greater is He who is within us than he who is in the world (see 1 John 4:4).

Do you want new wine? Do you want to fulfill God's destiny for you in this life? If you do, I recommend that you

- tune in to what the Spirit is saying to the churches,
- resolve to catch the wind of the Holy Spirit and
- agree to pay whatever price is necessary to become an active part of the new wineskin—including renewing your mind.

The new wineskin is the Second Apostolic Age. If you are a part of it, you can count yourself in the company of history makers!

ENDNOTES

Chapter One

1. Bill Hamon, *The Eternal Church*, rev. ed. (Shippensburg, PA: Destiny Image, 2003), p. 270.
2. David B. Barrett and Todd M. Johnson, "Annual Statistical Table of Global Mission," *International Bulletin of Missionary Research* (January 2003), p. 25. Barrett has assured the author in private correspondence (December 14, 2003) that the author's terminology and his refer to the same global phenomenon.
3. See David B. Barrett and Todd M. Johnson, *World Christian Trends, AD 30—AD 2200* (Pasadena, CA: William Carey Library, 2001), p. 302. The percentages are the author's calculations from the data presented.
4. Ibid., pp. 303-306.
5. Ibid., p. 293.
6. James Strong, *The New Strong's Exhaustive Concordance of the Bible* (Nashville, TN: Thomas Nelson Publishers, 1984), Hebrew ref. nos. 1080 and 1086.

Chapter Two

1. For more information on America as the seedbed of the denominational system, see Sidney E. Mead, "Denominationalism: The Shape of Protestantism in America," in *Denominationalism*, ed. Russell E. Richey (Nashville, TN: Abingdon Press, 1977), pp. 70-105.
2. 1949 Minutes of the General Council of the Assemblies of God, Resolution 7: "The New Order of the Latter Rain." Available from the Assemblies of God; 1445 Boonville Ave.; Springfield, MO 65802.
3. "Endtime Revival—Spirit-Led and Spirit-Controlled: A Response Paper to Resolution 16," adopted by General Presbytery, The General Council of the Assemblies of God, August 11, 2000, p. 2.
4. David Cartledge, *The Apostolic Revolution* (Chester Hill NSW, Australia: Paraclete Institute, 2000), pp. 236-242.
5. Martin E. Marty, "Chirping Season," *The Christian Century* (October 18, 2003), p. 63.
6. Ibid.
7. Jim Hodges, personal correspondence to author, February 8, 2004.

Chapter Three

1. See *Dictionary of Pentecostal and Charismatic Movements*, ed. Stanley M. Burgess and Gary B. McGee (Grand Rapids, MI: Zondervan Publishing House, 1988), s.v. "church growth."
2. Francis MacNutt, "Back to Our Roots," *The Healing Line* (March/April 2002), p. 5.
3. See Jennifer McKinney and Roger Finke, "Reviving the Mainline: An Overview of

Clergy Support for Evangelical Renewal Movements," *Journal for the Scientific Study of Religion*, vol. 41, no. 4 (2002), pp. 771-783.

4. Ibid., p. 771.
5. Michael S. Hamilton and Jennifer McKinney, "Turning the Mainline Around," *Christianity Today* (August 2003), p. 36.
6. Ibid., p. 40.
7. Ibid.
8. Joe Vatucicila, "Report from Fiji," personal correspondence, n.d.

Chapter Four

1. John R. W. Stott, "The Great Commission," in *One Race, One Gospel, One Task*, vol. 1, ed. Carl F. H. Henry and W. Stanley Mooneyham (Minneapolis, MN: World Wide Publications, 1967), p. 50.
2. John R. W. Stott, *Christian Mission in the Modern World* (Downers Grove, IL: InterVarsity Press, 1975), p. 35.
3. Ed Silvoso, *Anointed for Business* (Ventura, CA: Regal Books, 2002), p. 23.
4. David Oliver and James Thwaites, *Church That Works* (Milton Keynes, England: Word Publishing, 2001), p. 204.
5. Ibid., pp. 204-205.
6. Peter Tsukahira, *My Father's Business* (Haifa, Israel: Published by Peter Tsukahira, P.O. Box 7231, Haifa, Israel, 2000), p. 19.
7. The seed thoughts for this section on parachurch ministries came from Chris Hayward of Cleansing Stream Ministries.
8. James Thwaites, *Renegotiating the Church Contract* (Carlisle, England: Paternoster Press, 2001), p. ix.

Chapter Five

1. H. Richard Niebuhr, *The Social Sources of Denominationalism* (New York: The World Publishing Company, 1929), p. 25.
2. *Denominationalism*, ed. Russell E. Richey (Nashville, TN: Abingdon Press, 1977), p. 46.
3. Elwyn A. Smith, "The Forming of a Modern American Denomination," in *Denominationalism*, ed. Russell E. Richey, p. 135.
4. Joseph Mattera, "Apostles and Apostolic Movements," privately circulated paper, 2002, p. 2.
5. Ibid.
6. Ibid.

Chapter Six

1. Alistair Petrie, *Transformed! People, Cities, Nations: 10 Principles for Sustaining Genuine Revival* (Grand Rapids, MI: Chosen Books, 2003), p. 15.
2. Bob Weiner, *Take Dominion* (Old Tappan, NJ: Chosen Books, 1988), p. 153.

3. Ibid., p. 157.

4. Ibid., pp. 158-160.

5. Wesley Duewel, *Revival Fire* (Grand Rapids, MI: Zondervan Publishing House, 1995), p. 46.

6. Jackson Senyonga, "We Want It Quick, Big and Cheap," *Pray!* (July/August 2003), p. 36.

7. Wolfgang Simson, comp., *Friday Fax,* June 19, 2003, p. 1. *Friday Fax* is an e-mail sent only to subscribers; it is available by contacting FridayFax@bufton.net.

8. For more information on Almolonga, see George Otis, Jr., *Informed Intercession* (Ventura, CA: Renew Books, 1999), pp. 18-23; C. Peter Wagner, *Confronting the Powers* (Ventura, CA: Regal Books, 1996), pp. 217-220.

9. Os Hillman, "What Is Workplace Ministry?" *International Coalition of Workplace Ministries,* 2003-2004. http://www.icwm.net/articles_view.asp?articleid=606&col umnid= (accessed May 19, 2003).

Chapter Seven

1. John Eckhardt, *Moving in the Apostolic* (Ventura, CA: Renew Books, 1999), p. 64.

2. Chuck D. Pierce and Rebecca Wagner Sytsema, *The Future War of the Church* (Ventura, CA: Renew Books, 2001), p. 95.

3. John Kelly with Paul Costa, *End-Time Warriors* (Ventura, CA: Renew Books, 1999), p. 54.

4. Dale M. Sides, "An Apologia on Strategic Level Spiritual Warfare," *Episkopos* (August 2003), p. 4.

5. Ibid.

6. See, for example, C. Peter Wagner, "Probing History: 'Nothing New Under the Sun,'" in *Confronting the Powers* (Ventura, CA: Regal Books, 1996), pp. 91-120.

Chapter Eight

1. Christian A. Schwartz, *Natural Church Development* (Carol Stream, IL: ChurchSmart Resources, 1996), p. 23.

2. Ibid.

3. George Barna (directing leader of Barna Research Group, Ventura, CA), personal correspondence to author, 1998.

4. Barna Research Group, "Only Half of Protestant Pastors Have a Biblical Worldview," *Barna Research Online,* January 12, 2004. http://www.barna.org/cgi-bin/PagePressRelease.asp?PressReleaseID=156&Reference=F (accessed February 13, 2004).

5. Aubrey Malphurs, *Vision America* (Grand Rapids, MI: Baker Books, 1994), p. 192.

6. Leith Anderson, *A Church for the 21st Century* (Minneapolis, MN: Bethany House Publishers, 1992), p. 75.

7. Sidney E. Mead, "The Rise of the Evangelical Conception of the Ministry in America: 1607-1850" in *The Ministry in Historical Perspective,* ed. H. Richard Niebuhr and Daniel D. Williams (New York: Harper and Row, 1956), p. 242.

8. George Barna, personal correspondence to author, 1998.

9. Lyle E. Schaller, *The Senior Minister* (Nashville, TN: Abingdon Press, 1988), p. 84.

10. Paul Hattaway, et al, *Back to Jerusalem* (Waynesboro, GA: Gabriel Resources, 2003), p. xi.

11. See Robert Bellah, et al, *Habits of the Heart* (Berkeley, CA: University of California Press, 1985).

12. See Wade Clark Roof and William McKinney, *American Mainline Religion* (New Brunswick, NJ: Rutgers University Press, 1987), p. 244.

13. Andrew Strom, e-mail written March 31, 2003, from prophetic@revival.gen.nz.

14. See George Gallup, Jr., *The Unchurched American: 10 Years Later* (Princeton, NJ: Princeton Religion Research Center, 1988), p. 3.

Chapter Nine

1. See C. Peter Wagner, "Did Jesus Really Know?" *Evangelical Christian* (March 1959), n.p.; C. Peter Wagner, "Passing the Power," *How to Have a Healing Ministry in Any Church* (Ventura, CA: Regal Books, 1988), pp. 113-132.

2. Ted Haggard, *Dog Training, Fly Fishing, and Sharing Christ in the 21ˢᵗ Century* (Nashville, TN: Thomas Nelson Publishers, 2002), p. 108.

3. Ibid., pp. 109-110.

4. Ted Haggard, *Primary Purpose* (Orlando, FL: Creation House, 1995), p. 59.

5. Richard Foster, *Celebration of Discipline* (San Francisco: HarperSanFrancisco, 1988), p. 35.

6. John Sanders, "Does God Know Your Next Move?" *Christianity Today* (June 11, 2001), p. 52.

7. David Neff, "Open to Healing," *Christianity Today* (January 2004), pp. 21-22.

8. *The New International Dictionary of Pentecostal and Charismatic Movements*, ed. Stanley M. Burgess (Grand Rapids, MI: Zondervan Publishing House, 2002), s.v. "Oneness Pentecostalism."

9. For more information, see Talmadge L. French, *Our God Is One* (Indianapolis, IN: Voice and Vision, 1999), pp. 85-159.

Chapter Ten

1. *Webster's New Universal Unabridged Dictionary* (New York: Barnes and Noble Books, 1996), s.v. "inveterate."

2. George Barna, *The Second Coming of the Church* (Nashville, TN: Word Publishing, 1998), pp. 120-121.

SCRIPTURE INDEX

INDEX

More of the Best
from C. Peter Wagner

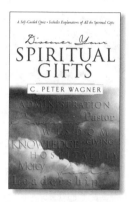

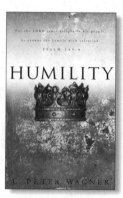

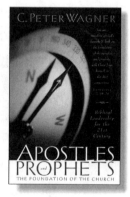

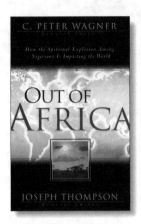
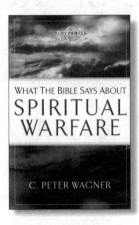

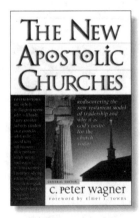
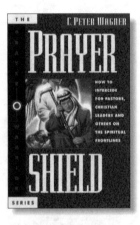
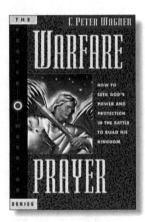